Published by:

**FPMI Communications, Inc.
707 Fiber St.
Huntsville, AL 35801-5833**

**(205) 539-1850
Fax: (205) 539-0911**

**Internet Address:
http://www.fpmi.com
e-mail: fpmi@fpmi.com**

*by G. Jerry Shaw and
Bill Bransford*

ISBN 0-936295-78-3

Table·Of
Contents

T a b l e · O f
C o n t e n t s

Forward

Numerous improvements have been made in this updated third edition. Many of them were suggested by readers of our previous editions, and those who attended our seminars. Thank you to those who took the time to suggest alterations.

Changes in legal interpretations by MSPB, EEOC and the courts were part of the reason for this third edition. The Vice President's National Performance Review recommendations were also partially responsible. (NPR materials cited this book and our workshop as support for some of their recommendations.) Most important was our continuing to see the necessity for supervisors, managers and executives to control the disruptive elements in their workforce at a time of great change, downsizing and new labor-management relationships. We sometimes find it necessary in our courses to tell supervisors, managers and executives that they are not in their positions for the purpose of being treated with disrespect. Nor are they employed to be the victims of those making unsubstantiated allegations to Inspectors General, the OSC, Congress and others in attempts to deflect responsibility for their own actions or failures. They are there to lead, encourage and "coach" their employees, and to stop those who have their own private goals from disrupting the workplace for those who are striving to effectively perform the government's business.

At least in part because of increased government training (and hopefully because of our book and seminar), we have seen an improvement in the willingness of supervisors, managers and executives to deal with problem employees. But, there is still a long way to go.

Sincerely,

G. Jerry Shaw
February, 1997

Preface

Failure to deal with problem employees is often not because of lack of will, but rather a lack of knowledge.

This book was many years in the making. Bill Bransford and I have each represented federal managers for more than 25 years, both while we were in the government and in private practice. During these years we came to realize that many federal managers are often on the receiving end of various allegations by subordinate employees. Many of these allegations are invalid, but the resulting investigations are the source of much worry and pain for managers, and even sometimes their families.

We discovered over time that allegations are often initiated by "problem" employees with whom the manager failed to deal. Such failure is often not because of a lack of will, but rather a lack of knowledge. The manager simply does not know how to handle an employee with a performance problem or, for example, one who is chronically tardy, or one who consistently abuses sick leave.

Often the manager tolerates the problem for a substantial period of time, so when he finally does take remedial steps, the employee believes that he or she is being singled out for improper purposes. By then it is often too late, and the seemingly endless cycle of charge and countercharge begins. The manager then pays the price by receiving poor performance ratings himself, and then he is the one seeking legal assistance.

Because of the numerous times we witnessed this cycle being repeated, we developed a course for managers on "How to Rehabilitate or Remove the Problem Employee." We have presented our course to hundreds of government managers since it was first offered in 1986.

Many managers attended the course when it was put on by the Senior Executives Association Professional Development League; others when their agencies had us provide the training. Unfortunately, the number we can reach through courses will always be limited, even though we continue to do this training. Recognizing this, we began writing this book in early 1991. After many re-writes, revisions and updates, we completed the First Edition in December, 1991. Additional refinements, revisions and updates to reflect changes in the law were made in the second edition and now in this third edition. Our hope is that this book provides federal managers with the basic legal principles which will allow them to deal effectively with problem employees.

We do not advocate the removal of employees, although the book does discuss termination situations. Rather, we firmly believe that early and swift intervention with a problem employee by a knowledgeable manager will allow correction of the problem and rehabilitation of the employee. This will allow the employee to continue his career as part of an efficient and effective government agency. It will also allow federal managers to do their work and provide leadership to their employees, rather than spend precious time and resources defending themselves against specious allegations. Of course, as the book points out, termination is sometimes necessary, but only after other efforts have proven fruitless.

Our plan is to update this book periodically, since the laws, rules, regulations and court decisions dealing with this topic constantly change. In addition, we know there probably are other areas we should cover in this book that we have not considered. Therefore, we welcome your comments and suggestions for future editions.

Please send them to FPMI Communications, Inc., 707 Fiber Street, Huntsville, AL 35801-5833. With your help, we can make this a book which will serve the goal of better government for all.

G. Jerry Shaw
February, 1997

P r e f a c e

Early and swift intervention with a problem employee will allow correction of the problem and rehabilitation of the employee.

Defining The Problem Employee

Defining The Problem Employee

Problem employees generally fit into three categories.

Efficiency Of The Service

The first step in dealing with a difficult personnel situation is to determine whether the supervisor actually has a problem employee. The best way to make this determination is by reference to the agency mission and the unit's goals. The Civil Service Reform Act of 1978 (CSRA) specifically gives management the right to define its mission. It also gives management the responsibility of communicating that mission to employees. (5 U.S.C. 4302 and 7106)

For example, if an agency's mission is to develop and promote decent housing for urban areas in the United States, the employee's role in carrying out that mission should be communicated to the employee through the position description, the performance plan containing critical elements and performance standards, and by periodic counseling with the supervisor. If the employee fails to carry out his role effectively after proper notice, the supervisor or manager can identify, evaluate and effectively rehabilitate or remove a person who has become a problem employee.

Problem employees generally fit into three categories: 1) employees who commit serious or repeated acts of misconduct, which are unacceptable in the workplace and cause a loss of efficiency if allowed to continue; 2) employees whose performance is unacceptable; and 3) employees who have committed no act of misconduct and who are working hard to meet performance standards but, for some reason through no fault of the employee, are unable to carry out the basic requirements of the job.

Category one covers misconduct cases, category two deals with performance, and category three cases are handled by utilizing the misconduct procedures outlined below. Separate systems have been developed by law and regulations within the federal government for handling misconduct and performance cases.

In determining whether an employee has committed an act of misconduct, the agency should first make an affirmative determination that the "efficiency of the service" is promoted by taking some action against an employee who has committed a particular infraction. "Efficiency of the service" is the statutory legal standard that all agencies must meet to support action against an employee who engages in misconduct. (5 U.S.C. 7503 and 7513)

One of the best ways to determine whether the efficiency of the service is promoted by discipline of some kind is by examining the agency rules or standards of conduct to the extent such rules exist. Other standards that could form the basis for adverse action are rules published by the Office of Government Ethics (5 C.F.R. Parts 2635 *et seq.*), and Title 18, United States Code (U.S.C.)(criminal violations). If a violation is of these rules or law, the efficiency of the service standard is generally met.

The supervisor should indicate in writing why he believes the efficiency of the service is promoted by taking an action against a particular employee. For example, a supervisor who is dealing with an employee who is often tardy can make a connection between the employee's tardiness and the work expectations of the unit. The efficiency of the service is promoted by taking action against a constantly tardy employee, so that the work may be completed.

In addition, if the employee's violation of the hours of work rules is tolerated, that may cause dissension among others who do follow the rules.

In many situations it is so obvious that misconduct hinders the efficiency of the service that articulation of a basis for agency action is quite easy. For example, fighting on the job with co-workers or destroying government property in a fit of anger would not require specific citations to published rules. However, in all cases the supervisor must be able to explain why the employee's actions justify disciplinary action that "promotes the efficiency" of the office.

Some federal agencies also have tables of penalties that prescribe specific penalties for various types of misconduct. A table of penalties is useful to a supervisor in selecting the appropriate penalty. For example, an agency may list insubordination in its table of penalties. The table may state what an appropriate penalty would be for a first offense. For example, it may state that an appropriate penalty is a written reprimand to a five-day suspension. The penalties that may be imposed for a second or third offense of insubordination would be more severe and would most likely include removal. Although there may be circumstances when the insubordination is so outrageous that the penalty of removal is appropriate for a first offense, the supervisor must specifically defend this choice of penalty after considering all the relevant factors in the case, since the removal penalty is not listed in the agency's table of penalties for a first offense.

> In many situations it is so obvious that misconduct hinders the efficiency of service that articulation of a basis for agency action is quite easy.

Critical Elements And Performance Standards

When an agency develops critical elements and performance standards for a particular job, the agency is defining its mission to the employee.

In fact, federal law requires that for each federal job an agency must develop written performance standards that are reasonably objective and attainable. (5 U.S.C. 4302) This does not mean that the standards must be completely objective.

A supervisor often must exercise his subjective judgment in appraising an employee's performance against the stated performance standards, and this is generally acceptable. However, the standards must reasonably put the employee on notice of what is expected of him and be capable of being utilized to adequately measure an employee's performance. If the employee is unclear about what his or her standards require, additional written and oral instructions by the supervisor can supplement the written performance standards. (See Chapter 10.)

Once valid performance standards are set by the agency, it is relatively easy for the supervisor to determine whether the agency has a problem employee. If the employee

Avoiding Allegations Of Prohibited Reprisal

A problem employee who uses complaint-filing activities as an offensive weapon can be a frustrating experience for a supervisor.

But, the supervisor is not powerless in this situation.

is not meeting the standards for acceptable performance, the employee is, by definition, a problem and must receive supervisory attention. If performance fails to improve, then the supervisor can take appropriate action.

In defining the problem employee, a supervisor or manager must be careful to avoid such considerations as the employee's filing of grievances, discrimination complaints or whistleblowing activity.

This can be a frustrating experience for federal supervisors, particularly if a problem employee uses the grievance procedure, discrimination complaint system, or whistleblowing activity to deflect attention from the problem employee's deficiencies.

Congress has decided that these complaint-filing activities are protected. Thus the efficiency of the service is not promoted by taking action against an employee as reprisal for filing grievances, Equal Employment Opportunity (EEO) complaints, or making lawfully protected disclosures.

A federal supervisor with an employee who uses this type of protected activity as an offensive weapon is not powerless, however, if the employee is also a problem employee because of performance or conduct problems. The manager must be careful, though, that this employee is treated the same as any other similarly situated employee who does not file complaints or grievances. The federal supervisor must assure that any personnel action taken against an employee who files complaints and grievances is based on legitimate management concerns and is not taken because of the complaints or grievances.

One way to establish that an action is legitimate as opposed to retaliatory is to compare the adverse action of an employee who engages in protected conduct with a similarly situated employee who also is subjected to an adverse action.

☑ CASE IN POINT

Two employees used a government computer for personal purposes. Employee A had filed numerous grievances against the supervisor while employee B had not. All other considerations being equal, both employees should receive the same penalty for their misconduct. If employee A is removed and employee B receives a reprimand, an inference can be drawn of unlawful reprisal by the supervisor, unless the difference in penalties is justified. cf. Hawkins v. Dep't. of Navy, 49 M.S.P.R. 501 (1991).

Another means of avoiding allegations of reprisal is to examine precedents from the Merit Systems Protection Board (MSPB) which have sustained disciplinary actions for similar misconduct or non-performance. Federal supervisors should respect the rights of employees to file grievances, but they should also insist that during work hours the employee must be doing his job (with appropriate allowance for official time to prepare or present complaints and grievances when required).

The MSPB upheld an adverse action directed against an employee who submitted a false and malicious statement about a supervisor in connection with an EEO complaint; see *Johnson v. Dep't. of the Army,* 48 M.S.P.R. 54 (1991), *aff'd,* 960 F.2d 156 (Fed. Cir. 1992). Thus, there are limits to what an employee can do in pursuing an EEO or other protected complaint. Regardless, care must be taken to ensure that the real reason for the adverse action in such situations is the false statement, not the fact that the employee has named the supervisor in an EEO complaint or filed a grievance against the supervisor.

Too often a personnel decision is motivated by a personal or emotional reaction toward a subordinate employee. While these reactions sometimes may be justified, a rational and careful evaluation of an employee's conduct or performance to determine how, if at all, that performance or conduct affects the agency's mission is the proper basis to use for proposing an adverse action. This attitude, coupled with careful application of the procedures outlined in the following chapters, will help assure success in rehabilitating problem employees.

Too often a personnel decision is motivated by a personal or emotional reaction toward an employee.

Recognizing and Handling Employee Misconduct

Recognizing And Handling Employee Misconduct Identifying

Federal law authorizes an agency to take disciplinary action against a federal employee who engages in misconduct, either on or off the worksite. (5 U.S.C. 7503 and 7513.) Before taking an adverse action against an employee for misconduct, a federal supervisor should consider three basic issues. First, the agency should identify the conduct warranting discipline or adverse action. Second, once the conduct is identified, the agency should establish a "nexus" or connection between the employee's misconduct and the employee's work for the federal government and the agency. Third, the agency should choose the appropriate discipline to be imposed based on the misconduct identified. (The issue of appropriate penalty is examined in detail in Chapter 5.)

The Type Of Misconduct

In identifying employee misconduct, the agency's first task is to distinguish between actual misconduct and a problem with an employee's performance. An employee's job performance is evaluated by reference to specific critical elements and job standards developed under the procedures set forth in Chapter 43 of Title 5, United States Code and Parts 430 and 432 of Title 5, Code of Federal Regulations. A serious one-time performance problem, such as causing a threat to life or property may, however, justify a conduct adverse action.

An employee's misconduct must be identified as actual conduct or a problem with the employee's performance.

On the other hand, a routine, one-time, non-adherence to job standards, such as failure to submit a report in a timely manner, would warrant the second chance required by the performance system. (Processing performance adverse actions is examined in Chapters 8 through 12.)

Otherwise, an employee's conduct is evaluated against each agency's standards of conduct. An adverse action may be taken against an employee if the action meets the statutory requirement of promoting the efficiency of the service. (5 U.S.C. 7513(a)) The Merit Systems Protection Board gave meaning to this statutory standard in *Hatfield v. Dep't. of the Interior,* 28 M.S.P.R. 673 (1985). There, the MSPB found that an adverse action promotes the efficiency of the service when grounds for the adverse action relate either to the employee's ability to accomplish his duties satisfactorily or to some other legitimate government interest.

The efficiency of the service is not promoted, for example, by bringing charges against an employee because the employee filed an Equal Employment Opportunity (EEO) complaint or grievance. (See Chapters 6, 13 and 19 on reprisal as a prohibited personnel practice.) Also, in taking an adverse action the agency bears the burden of proving that the employee's misconduct affects the efficiency of the service; see *Johnson v. Dep't. of Health and Human Services,* 22 M.S.P.R. 521 (1984). If the employee appeals the adverse action to the MSPB, the agency must meet its burden of proof by a "preponderance of the evidence." (5 C.F.R. 1201.56(a)(ii))

The MSPB has defined the evidentiary standard of "preponderance of the evidence" to mean that the agency must prove the facts in its case by that degree of evidence which a reasonable mind, considering the record as a whole, would accept as sufficient to find that the fact asserted is more likely true than not; see *Hilderbrand v. Dep't. of Justice,* 22 M.S.P.R. 233 (1984).

Conversely, the employee has no burden of disproving the charges, i.e., an employee's failure to deny the charges does not relieve the agency of its ultimate burden to prove its case; *see Gary v. Veterans Administration,* 19 M.S.P.R. 247 (1984). For this reason the agency must satisfy its obligation by submitting a well-developed record to the MSPB in order to prove its case by a preponderance of the evidence.

The agency's record should demonstrate by a preponderance of the evidence that the misconduct alleged by the agency has in fact occurred and that the adverse action taken will promote the efficiency of the service; *see Kendrick v. Veterans Administration,* 11 M.S.P.R. 617 (1982).

The evidentiary standard of proof in a conduct case differs from that applied in a performance-based adverse action. In the latter, the standard of proof is by "substantial evidence." (5 C.F.R. 1201.56(a)(i)) The substantial evidence standard is a lower standard of proof than the preponderance of the evidence standard. (See Chapter 8.) Thus, the standard of proof in a conduct case places a greater burden on the agency; *see Flood v. Dep't. of the Navy,* 19 M.S.P.R. 163 (1984).

> An employee's failure to deny charges does not relieve the agency of its burden to prove its case.

Establishing A Nexus Between The Misconduct And The Employee's Position

As part of its burden in justifying an adverse action based on misconduct, the agency must demonstrate a clear and direct relationship between the grounds for the action and the employee's ability to perform his duties satisfactorily, the agency's ability to fulfill its assigned mission, or some other legitimate government interest promoting the efficiency of the service; *see Burkwist v. Dep't. of Transportation,* 26 M.S.P.R. 427 (1985).

While the MSPB requires an agency to establish a direct relationship, it does not require an agency to demonstrate a specific impact on an employee's job performance or service efficiency to establish a nexus. It is enough if an agency establishes that public perception of an employee's misconduct would impair the efficiency of the agency by undermining public confidence and thereby impeding the ability of its other employees to perform effectively.

☑ CASE IN POINT

A GS-4 secretary on an Air Force base located in the Philippines engaged in off-duty misconduct related to black marketing of motor vehicles. The employee was the ringleader who solicited other agency personnel to engage in the black market scheme, which involved, in part, falsification of the agency's records in order to conceal the improper transfer of the motor vehicles. The MSPB found sufficient evidence to show that the employee's conduct adversely affected the agency's trust and its confidence in his ability to perform his duties in a proper manner, particularly since the employee had access to personnel files and sensitive information and since his job required contact with the public. Thus, even though the employee's activities were not directly related to his job, the MSPB found sufficient nexus to permit an adverse action; see Jordan v. Dep't. of the Air Force, 36 M.S.P.R. 409, 414-415 (1988), aff'd, 884 F.2d 1398 (Fed. Cir. 1989), cert. denied, 493 U.S. 1061 (1990).

> An employee's off-duty misconduct may also be grounds for disciplinary action if the conduct relates to the employee's position.

An employee's off-duty misconduct may also be grounds for disciplinary action if the conduct relates to the employee's position. The MSPB has recognized three methods by which an agency may show a nexus between off-duty misconduct and the efficiency of the service.

• First, if the employee commits a serious act of off-duty misconduct, the agency may be entitled to a presumption that there is a nexus between the misconduct and the efficiency of the service. For example, if the employee engaged in an assault with a deadly weapon where violence or force is an integral part of the conduct, there is a presumption of connection or "nexus" with the employee's job. The employee could, however, defeat or rebut the presumption by proving that no such connection existed.

• Second, the agency may show that the misconduct adversely affected: a) the employee's or a co-worker's performance, and/or b) the agency's trust and confidence in the employee's performance.

• Third, the agency may show that the misconduct interfered with or otherwise adversely affected the agency's mission.

☑ CASE IN POINT

A Postal Service letter carrier pled guilty to statutory rape of a 14-year-old girl. In his defense the employee stated that the girl had lied to him about her age, claiming the girl was 16, the age of consent. The employee claimed that the girl was a neighbor and that all relations between them occurred at his home, with her consent, and without any force or threat. On this basis, the MSPB found that the employee's misconduct did not involve violence or force and thus, the agency was not entitled to rely on only a presumption of nexus. Further, the agency produced no testimony of any co-workers who objected to his continued employment, nor evidence that the employee came in contact with young girls in the performance of his duties. Finally, the MSPB found that nothing about the employee's misconduct interfered with the agency's mission. The agency in this case therefore relied on the presumption of nexus but the employee was able to defeat or rebut the presumption by proving a nexus did not exist. Since the agency did not produce other evidence, it did not meet its burden of proof on the issue of nexus and the proposed removal was not sustained; see Moten v. U.S. Postal Service, 42 M.S.P.R. 282 (1989). *However, in* Graham v. U.S. Postal Service, 49 M.S.P.R. 364 (1991), *the MSPB accepted the presumption of nexus raised by the agency where a postal worker was convicted of sexual abuse of a 14-year-old girl, and the worker failed to prove that a nexus did not exist.*

In summary, a supervisor may take disciplinary action against an employee who engages in misconduct if such action promotes the efficiency of the service. The supervisor should develop a record that demonstrates that it is more likely true than not that the misconduct alleged has occurred, and that the adverse action relates either to the employee's ability to accomplish his duties or to another legitimate government interest. Once these determinations are made, the supervisor is ready to choose the appropriate penalty to be imposed for the misconduct.

Documenting And Proving A Misconduct Case

Documenting And Proving A Misconduct Case

It is crucial that the agency document in writing both the employee's misconduct and the action taken by the agency once the misconduct is discovered.

In the federal workplace, each agency has an affirmative obligation to assist its employees when their work is adversely affected by misconduct, poor performance, or both. This means that in cases where the employee's performance is not acceptable, the agency should make a genuine effort to help the employee rather than acting automatically to replace him.

In minor misconduct cases (e.g., tardiness), the agency, through the appropriate supervisor, should bring the matter to the attention of the employee and take appropriate corrective action immediately. Ideally, the employee should be able successfully to continue his career after any necessary discipline has been imposed. If, however, the employee's misconduct is so serious that immediate removal or suspension is both justified and necessary because of the type of conduct involved (e.g., stealing from petty cash), the supervisor should contact the agency's personnel office. If necessary the Inspector General's office, which has authority to investigate and establish a record that documents suspected serious misconduct, should be asked to investigate. The supervisor then should act on the advice of the appropriate agency officials.

In some cases the employee may challenge the agency's action by asserting that the misconduct did not occur, that his actions were justified or minor, or that the agency's reaction to the employee's misconduct was unreasonable. In order to withstand such a challenge, it is crucial that the agency document in writing both the employee's misconduct and the action taken by the agency once the misconduct is discovered. Written documentation will help assure that the supervisor's actions are supported at a higher level within the agency or in another forum, such as the Merit Systems Protection Board (MSPB) or the Equal Employment Opportunity Commission (EEOC).

The agency's record should include documentation reflecting the nature of the misconduct, when it occurred, and how the agency discovered it.

Reasons For Documenting A Case

In cases where an employee is disciplined for misconduct, the employee may challenge the agency's action informally, such as through the agency's grievance process or through the agency's adverse action procedures, or he may initiate a formal challenge before the MSPB or in the courts. In the face of a challenge the agency must demonstrate that the charges on which the disciplinary action is based are supported by a preponderance of the evidence. This means that the deciding official or judge must be convinced that it is more likely than not that the events surrounding the misconduct occurred as the agency depicts them; *see Jackson v. Veterans Administration,* 768 F.2d 1325 (Fed. Cir. 1985); *Johnson v. Dep't. of the Air Force,* 13 M.S.P.R. 236 (1982). The more fully a case is documented, the more likely the agency will prevail.

Another reason for carefully documenting a case is to allow supervisors, witnesses and other employees to use the documentation prepared at the time the misconduct occurred to refresh their memory at a later time, should they be called to testify about the matter.

Given the number of employees under a manager's supervision at any particular time, it is unreasonable to expect each supervisor and co-worker to recall the specific details surrounding each and every action taken by each and every employee. Certainly witnesses may not recall specific details of an event if called upon to recount them at a hearing months later. Accordingly, a prudent supervisor should make an immediate written notation to the file when he observes or discovers inappropriate conduct by an employee.

Documentation recorded contemporaneously (i.e., as close as possible to the time misconduct is observed or discovered) is much more reliable than records prepared long after-the-fact. Documentation prepared later could be perceived as being "created" by a supervisor to build a case against an employee for inappropriate reasons. Moreover, contemporaneous documentation will be given substantial weight and probative value as evidence at a hearing, especially if the statements in the memorandum or notes are unchallenged by the employee or corroborated by independent sources; *see Rodriguez v. Dep't. of Agriculture,* 27 M.S.P.R. 79 (1985); *Gamble v. Dep't. of the Army,* 23 M.S.P.R. 11 (1984). If there is a conflict regarding what occurred at a meeting, contemporaneous notes may make the difference in a credibility determination (i.e., determining who is telling the truth); *see Wright v. Dep't. of Transportation,* 24 M.S.P.R. 550 (1984).

Another benefit of documenting employee misconduct is that the documentation can be used when the agency provides the employee notice that it believes a problem exists and what it perceives the problem to be. This notice to the employee may be optional, depending on agency regulations or applicable collective bargaining agreements. However, furnishing documentation prepared at the time of the event to the employee can help establish the agency's good faith in showing that an attempt was made to rehabilitate the employee.

Finally, in the event that an adverse action is necessary, effective documentation serves two purposes. First, it can assist in the preparation of a detailed proposal notice. (See Chapter 7.) The MSPB has indicated that a proposal notice may have weight as evidence if the notice provides a sufficiently detailed account of the events on which the adverse action is based and if the notice is corroborated by documentary evidence; *see Gill v. Dep't. of the Navy,* 34 M.S.P.R. 308 (1987).

Second, documentation may be used in compiling the agency file, which the agency is required to prepare and provide to the MSPB in response to an employee appeal of an agency action. (5 C.F.R. 1201.25) This "agency file" becomes part of the administrative record of an MSPB appeal and constitutes evidence at an MSPB hearing. Similarly, in the context of an EEO case, detailed documentation may be provided to support the reasons for agency action in the investigative stages of the EEO complaint process. The documentation also becomes part of the administrative file in the event of an EEO hearing where the employee challenges the agency action.

> The more fully a case is documented, the more likely the agency will prevail.

How To
Document
A Case

Documentation of

meetings with a

problem employee

need not be formal

and may be simply

a brief, handwrit-

ten note.

When documenting a case, the agency should retain all important and relevant written evidence of the employee's misconduct. This includes evidence that shows the misconduct occurred, as well as proof of what action the agency took and the reasons why the action was justified.

The agency must make sure that such written evidence is also provided to its personnel office to be placed in a file along with the notice of proposed disciplinary action, especially if the information is to be relied upon as a basis for proposing disciplinary action. (See Chapter 7.)

Each time the supervisor has a meeting with a problem employee about misconduct, the supervisor should draft a written memorandum to the file detailing what occurred at the meeting. This memorandum need not always be formal and may be simply a brief, handwritten note. All other employees having significant information concerning the employee's misconduct should also be asked to prepare similar memoranda.

Such memoranda are important for three reasons:

1) they provide a written record of how the agency handled the problem;

2) they assist each person who drafted a memorandum in refreshing his recollection if called to testify concerning his knowledge of the facts; and

3) they serve as evidence to corroborate that a conference or counseling session between an employee and supervisor took place, in the event the employee denies it or disputes what happened.

As noted above, such notes may also be considered probative evidence in the event of an MSPB appeal on the adverse action.

The manner in which documentation is accomplished is not important. Rather, it is only important that significant and pertinent information is recorded in some retrievable fashion. For example, supervisors can record a meeting or an employee's tardiness or absence on a desk calendar, adding just a few phrases alongside the notation. Such a system might be used to document significant events with all employees, not just a problem employee.

Documentation can also be accomplished by keeping a specific log book on a particular employee. While some supervisors may react negatively to the idea of "keeping book" on someone, this is a permissible practice and, in fact, enhances the likelihood that the agency would prevail in an adverse action against an employee.

Many agencies maintain "drop" or supervisors' files. These are files in which both positive and negative information is routinely maintained on an employee. If drop files are maintained, supervisors can include quick notes, even on scratch paper, which indicate the date, time, and significant aspects of a particular event. Note that some collective bargaining agreements require that such notations, log books, etc., be provided to the employee when made.

Use Of Documentation For One-On-One Situations

When employee misconduct cannot be resolved informally, an accurate written record enhances an agency's success in court or before the MSPB or EEOC.

A common fallacy in the federal workplace is that one-on-one conversations are off-the-record or cannot later be relied upon to support disciplinary or adverse actions.

The agency need only prove a misconduct case by a preponderance of the evidence. This means that the agency must prove that the charges are more likely true than not true. While it is obvious that one person's word against another person's word may be insufficient evidence to establish charges by a preponderance, the MSPB often will credit a supervisor's testimony and discredit a subordinate's testimony about the same incident because it presumes the supervisor has less interest in lying, distorting the facts, or perceiving the events incorrectly than does the employee who is being subjected to an adverse action; *see Hillen v. Dep't. of the Army*, 35 M.S.P.R. 453 (1987) (general credibility factors considered by MSPB).

When a supervisor has an encounter with an employee that may later become the subject of an adverse action or a significant factor in an adverse action, the supervisor's contemporaneous notes about the event are important pieces of evidence. The fact that a contemporaneous note was prepared and that a supervisor's testimony is consistent with that note provides additional support for crediting the supervisor's testimony. Under these circumstances, the agency should, in most instances, be able to establish by a preponderance of the evidence that a particular event occurred, even if the only witnesses to the event are the supervisor and the employee. This is one of the most important reasons for effective documentation by a supervisor.

The next several chapters provide guidance in cases where the employee's differences with the agency cannot be resolved informally. In such cases, a careful and accurate written record will enhance the agency's likelihood of success in supporting its actions in court or before the MSPB or EEOC.

Common Types Of Misconduct

Common Types Of Misconduct

Employee misconduct which justifies a supervisor's consideration of an adverse action takes many forms. The case decisions of the Merit Systems Protection Board (MSPB) list hundreds of different types of misconduct. The only requirement is that some showing be made that in taking the adverse action the efficiency of the service will be promoted. The supervisor need not fit the misconduct into a specific title when notifying the employee of the misconduct, and no limitation exists on the number or types of misconduct that can be charged. This differs from criminal law where a person's misconduct must fit into pre-determined prohibitions.

As discussed in Chapter 2, misconduct that occurs outside the workplace and beyond regular duty hours may warrant an adverse action if there is a sufficient "nexus" between the conduct and the employee's position. On the other hand, some employee conduct, such as failure to maintain a security clearance, is not misconduct, but may nevertheless form the basis for an adverse action against the employee.

The more common types of employee misconduct warranting disciplinary or adverse action are discussed below. These should not be considered as limitations but rather as examples of misconduct issues previously litigated at the MSPB.

Attendance-Related Charges

- Tardiness

- Absence Without Leave

- Sick Leave Abuse

• Tardiness
Tardiness is a common and minor type of attendance-related misconduct. Problems arising from an employee who is late for work or who is late in returning from a lunch break may usually be handled by an oral counseling session or a written reprimand. Repeated instances of tardiness, however, may warrant more severe disciplinary action. Failure to deal with repeated tardiness can destroy workplace morale.

• Absence Without Leave (AWOL)
To support an adverse action against an employee based on "AWOL," the agency must demonstrate that the employee was absent and that the absence was not authorized, or that the employee's request for leave had been denied. Because no agency is expected to tolerate repeated instances of AWOL by an employee, nexus is presumed. An employee may attempt to defend an action based on AWOL by claiming that a mental or physical illness affected the employee's ability to attend work. The burden is on the employee to prove this alleged illness and its effect upon the employee's ability to attend work. AWOL is a serious offense and penalties such as lengthy suspensions and even removal are commonly upheld by the MSPB.

☑ CASE IN POINT
An employee was removed by his agency on charges that he: 1) failed to return to his job site after a training class was dismissed, 2) had unexcused tardiness on three occasions, and 3) had unauthorized absence without leave (AWOL) on three occasions. The employee defended one instance of AWOL claiming that he was physically and mentally exhausted by his heavy workload and harassment by his supervisor. The employee also claimed that his condition prevented him from going to see a doctor and therefore, he was

unable to provide a medical certification for his absence. On appeal from the agency removal, the MSPB held that the employee submitted insufficient medical documentation to support his claim that his AWOL was the result of his physical and mental exhaustion. The Board also held that there was insufficient evidence of harassment by the employee's supervisor. However, after examination of all of the evidence, the Board upheld only the charges of one day of unauthorized absence and three instances of tardiness.

Nevertheless, the Board determined that the penalty of removal was reasonable, even when based on the reduced charges; see Pope v. Dep't. of Navy, 44 M.S.P.R. 289 (1990).

• Sick Leave Abuse

An agency is obligated to grant sick leave to an employee when the employee:

1) receives medical, dental or optical examinations or treatment;

2) is incapacitated for the performance of duty by sickness, injury, or pregnancy and confinement;

3) is required to give care and attention to a member of his immediate family who is sick, injured, pregnant, or in need of a medical exam;

4) would jeopardize the health of others by his presence at the workplace because of exposure to a contagious disease;

5) arranges or attends the funeral of a family member; or

6) must be absent to engage in activities necessary for the adoption of a child. (5 C.F.R. 630.401)

In order for a request for sick leave to be approved, the employee must file a written application for sick leave within such period of time that the agency may prescribe. The agency may grant sick leave only when supported by evidence that is "administratively acceptable." (5 C.F.R. 603.403) The burden to provide this administratively acceptable evidence in support of the sick leave request is upon the employee making the request. An agency is under no obligation to approve leave unless the leave is requested and supported by a valid basis; *see Barner v. U.S. Postal Service,* 11 M.S.P.R. 357 (1982). While most federal employees have a right to use accrued sick leave if they are incapacitated, this right does not apply to postal service employees. (See Chapter 18.) Also, even federal employees who have accrued sick leave do not enjoy unlimited rights to lengthy absences from critical positions.

If a supervisor becomes concerned that an employee is using an excessive amount of sick leave or if the evidence in support of a sick leave request is inadequate, the supervisor may consider placing the employee on a "leave restriction notice."

> Employee misconduct which justifies a supervisor's consideration of an adverse action takes many forms.

Abuse of leave

is reason for

discplinary action

up to and includ-

ing removal.

A typical leave restriction notice provides the employee notice that sick leave will not be granted unless the employee is able to provide a medical certificate. An employee who fails to provide the appropriate documentation, whether in support of a simple request for sick leave or as required under a leave restriction letter, may be disciplined. Abuse of leave is reason for disciplinary action up to and including removal.

In addition to sick leave, federal employees are now entitled to Family and Medical Leave. This entitles employees to a total of 12 administrative workweeks of unpaid leave during any 12 month period for any of the following reasons:

1) the birth and care of the employee's child;

2) the placement of a child with an employee through adoption or foster care;

3) the care of an immediate family member with a "serious health condition"; or

4) a "serious health condition" of the employee that makes the employee unable to per-form his or her job. (5 C.F.R. 630.1203(a))

An employee may elect, however, to substitute accrued annual or sick leave for any or all of the Family and Medical Leave period taken under this OPM regulation. (5 C.F.R. 630.1205) An employee's election to substitute annual or sick leave for unpaid Family and Medical Leave must be consistent with current laws and regulations governing the granting and use of such leave. Id.

If an employee fails to comply with leave use procedures, the supervisor may appropri-ately place the employee in an AWOL status. Discipline may then be initiated against the employee on the basis of the charges of sick leave abuse and AWOL. To support an adverse action based upon sick leave abuse and AWOL, the agency should be prepared to demon-strate that the employee either did not request leave, or that the medical certificate he submitted to the agency failed to provide sufficient medical basis for the employee's ab-sence.

☑ CASE IN POINT

Ernest received an unsatisfactory attendance (leave restriction) letter from his agency, which advised that he needed to submit valid certificates from attending physicians to obtain sick leave. The agency advised Ernest that failure to follow the proper procedures for requesting sick leave would result in his being charged AWOL. The agency also notified him that, if necessary, disciplinary action would be taken to correct the situation. Ernest called in on April 1st to say that he had car trouble and to request leave. Ernest called in sick on April 9th, 11th, and 15th, and did not return to work until April 30th. The agency placed Ernest in an AWOL status because he had failed to follow the proper procedures for requesting leave. The MSPB upheld Ernest's removal from his agency on the basis that the agency proved by preponderant evidence that it did not abuse its discretion in denying Ernest sick leave between April 1st and April 30th.

Ernest was on notice through the leave restriction letter that failure to follow the proper procedures for requesting leave would result in AWOL. Ernest made no attempt to comply with these procedures and could therefore be disciplined; see Morris v. Dep't. of Air Force, 30 M.S.P.R. 343 (1986).

Until recently, an agency was precluded from charging an employee with failure to follow leave-requesting procedures when it subsequently granted an employee's leave; *see Yartzoff v. E.P.A.,* 38 M.S.P.R. 403, 407 (1988). Thus, an agency, had to place an employee in an AWOL status as a condition to charging an employee with failure to follow leave-requesting procedures. The MSPB recently lifted this preclusion and has authorized federal agencies to charge an employee with failure to properly request sick leave, annual leave, or leave without pay, even though the agency eventually approves the employee's leave request; *see Wilkinson v. Dep't. of Air Force,* 68 M.S.P.R. 4,7 (1995). In lifting the ban and allowing agencies to charge leave abuses without disapproving the underlying leave, the MSPB rationalized that it will encourage agencies "to grant compelling leave requests," while allowing agencies "to hold employees accountable for their failure to follow proper leave-requesting procedures." Id.

> If an employee fails to comply with leave use procedures, he could be placed in an AWOL status.

Insubordination

• Elements of Insubordination

In the most basic sense, insubordination is the intentional and willful refusal to follow a supervisor's order, an order that the supervisor is entitled to have obeyed. A charge of insubordination will be upheld against an employee if the employee's supervisor gives a valid order which the employee refuses to obey. The operative word is refusal; it is not sufficient that the employee failed to follow the order out of ignorance or merely delayed following a supervisor's orders. Thus, some excuses proffered by employees for their refusal to follow an order may reverse the charge of insubordination. For example, an employee who is unable to perform work may not be guilty of insubordination. An employee who is too sick to work is also not insubordinate. Similarly, an employee who attempts, but does not comply with instructions is not insubordinate.

> A charge of insubordination will be upheld against an employee if the employee's supervisor gives a valid order which the employee refuses to obey.

☑ CASE IN POINT

An agency suspended an employee for 45 days for failing to follow instructions that he remain by the telephone for a specific period so that the employee would be accessible by either telephone or pager. The MSPB sent this case back for further review to resolve the factual issue of the possibility that the employee wore the pager but it failed to function for reasons beyond the employee's knowledge or control.

If the pager had not functioned properly as the employee contended, the employee would have been unable to respond to the pager, and could not be found to be insubordinate; see Allen v. Dep't. of Agriculture, 37 M.S.P.R. 234 (1988).

Because the agency must prove a case of insubordination by demonstrating that the employee intentionally failed to follow an order, the employee may attempt to defend the action by claiming that he did not understand. This may be an effective defense in that an employee is not insubordinate if his conduct was not willful. In the absence of intent, an

> If an employee is given an order and takes issue with it, he should perform the work first and grieve about it later.

agency may charge an employee with failure to follow supervisory instructions, which is distinct from insubordination because it does not require proof of intentional and willful disobedience. *Hamilton v. U.S.P.S.,* 1996 WL 593834 (M.S.P.B.).

The second element of the charge of insubordination is that the employee was given an order. If the order to perform is unclear, however, a charge of insubordination may not be sustained. On the other hand, an employee's receipt of explicit notification (e.g., that his driving privileges were revoked for driving an automobile on the military base) fully puts the employee on notice of the order, and the agency can expect that the order will be obeyed; *see Thias v. Dep't. of Air Force,* 32 M.S.P.R. 46 (1986).

• "Obey Now, Grieve Later" Principle and Its Applicability to Insubordination
Related to the issue of insubordination is the general rule that all employees "obey now, grieve later." This means that if an employee is given an order to perform certain work, he should perform that work. If he takes issue with the order to perform his work, he should do the work first and grieve about it later. In summary, an employee's refusal to work, even if the employee believes he has a valid reason, may be viewed as insubordination.

☑ CASE IN POINT
A correctional officer at a U.S. penitentiary was charged with insubordination when an agency official who was conducting an inspection of the employee's post in a guard tower observed that the employee's totebag contained reading material. Written agency policy prohibited reading material in a guard tower. The supervisor asked the employee about the contents of the totebag and ordered the employee to allow a search of the bag. The employee refused to allow the search until he received notice from a higher-level agency official that the search was authorized. The employee was removed from his position for insubordination on the grounds that he refused to allow the search of his totebag and made disrespectful comments toward his supervisors. The MSPB upheld the removal of the employee, noting that the employee should not have refused to obey orders to allow a search of his totebag. The employee did not have the unfettered right to disregard an order merely because the employee believed it to be an improper order; see Ingram v. Dep't. of Justice, 44 M.S.P.R. 578 (1990).

An exception to the obey now, grieve later rule is a situation where following an order will place the employee in a dangerous situation; for example, if the employee will risk serious injury to himself by complying with the orders of his supervisor; *see Blocker v. Dep't. of the Army;* 6 M.S.P.R. 467 (1981). (An order to an employee to take a car through a car wash and wax another car is not the type of threat to an employee's health and well-being, even considering the employee's back condition, which would excuse an employee's refusal to work.) Another exception is that an employee will not be considered insubordinate for failing to submit to an improperly ordered psychiatric examination.

In the situation of random, mandatory drug testing, the failure of an employee in a public, safety-oriented position to submit to such testing may properly result in his removal, regardless of the constitutionality of random drug resting in the federal workforce; *see Watson v. Dep't. of Transportation,* No. 91-3558, 1991 WL 336951 (Fed. Cir. Nov. 18, 1991) (sustaining removal of air traffic controller despite employee's reliance on federal appeals court case declaring random, mandatory drug resting unconstitutional).

The rule of law applied in such cases is that, "absent circumstances where compliance would involve clear physical danger, regulations and laws must be obeyed, even if unconstitutional, unless obedience would prevent a subsequent legal challenge." Thus, there exists no "unconstitutionality" exception to the obey now, grieve later principle.

It should be noted that the agency must prove that the employee deliberately and willfully refused to follow an order. An employee's disagreement with a supervisor, if the employee does not refuse to work, is not necessarily insubordination.

A related exception to the obey now, grieve later principle is an employee's refusal to violate a law. It is a prohibited personnel practice for an agency to take action against an employee who refuses to obey an order that would require him or her to violate a law. (See chapter 6.) A word of caution is necessary here, since an employee who refuses to follow such an order acts at his or her own risk and assumes that to obey the order would actually result in violation of a law. That assessment is not always clear-cut.

An employee's delay in complying with an order, if the employee is attempting to follow the order, does not rise to the level of insubordination; *see Phillips v. General Services Administration,* 878 F.2d 370 (Fed. Cir. 1989).

On the other hand, disagreement with a supervisor as to what is required by the employee's position description is not an excuse justifying insubordination.

• Disrespectful Behavior Toward Supervisors
Supervisors must be careful to distinguish between insubordination and disrespectful behavior. Disrespectful behavior is a related but less serious offense than insubordination. Nonetheless, it is one for which an adverse action may be taken.

☑ CASE IN POINT
Owen, an employee of the Dep't. of the Navy, was orally reprimanded by his supervisor when it appeared he was taking an extended lunch period. Several minutes later, Owen entered his supervisor's work area and, in the presence of several other of the supervisor's subordinates, purposely spoke in a loud voice so that others could hear him stating that the supervisor's actions were anti-Semitic, that the supervisor had no right to treat him like a dog, that the supervisor acted toward him like a Nazi prison guard, and that the supervisor was worse than a Gestapo agent. Although the employee's conduct was not insubordinate per se, in that the employee did not refuse to follow an order, the employee knowingly made malicious statements with the intent of harming the reputation and authority of his supervisor. The MSPB upheld a 20-day suspension as an appropriate penalty for this type of disrespectful conduct; see Scheer v. Dep't. of Navy, 34 M.S.P.R. 529 (1987).

> An agency must prove that the employee deliberately and willfully refused to follow an order.

Criminal Charges

The decision whether to treat criminal conduct as a crime or misconduct rests with the agency.

In conclusion, the supervisor should define the employee's conduct correctly before determining the appropriate penalty. Although insubordination and disrespectful conduct have some similarities, they are two different types of misconduct warranting different types of penalties.

Supervisors should only charge subordinates with insubordination if they can point specifically to a lawful instruction that the subordinate refused to carry out.

An agency may, under some circumstances, take disciplinary action against an employee, including removal, because the employee has engaged in criminal activity for which criminal charges are pending. The following discussion examines an agency's rights when an employee is actually charged with a crime, or when the agency wishes to focus on the criminality of the employee's conduct.

The decision whether to treat criminal conduct as a crime or misconduct rests with the agency. For example, an employee who physically threatens a supervisor may have committed a crime under most state criminal codes, but the agency may choose to disregard the criminal nature of the employee's misconduct. Discussions in other sections of this chapter mention employee misconduct which technically could be a crime.

If the criminal activity occurs off-duty, the agency must demonstrate a nexus between the employee's criminal activity and his position. The agency may indefinitely suspend an employee pending disposition of serious criminal charges against him if conviction on the charges could bring a sentence of imprisonment. (5 C.F.R. 752.402(e))

☑ CASE IN POINT

An agency indefinitely suspended an employee from his position as an electrician pending the disposition of criminal charges against the employee for involuntary deviate sexual behavior, unlawful restraint, corruption of minors, indecent assault, indecent exposure, endangering the welfare of a child, aggravated assault, simple assault, and open lewdness. The MSPB upheld the indefinite suspension, finding that the agency showed by a preponderance of the evidence that there was reasonable cause to believe that the employee committed the crimes and that the suspension would terminate upon the disposition of the criminal charges against the employee. The MSPB also found that a nexus existed between the offenses charged and the employee's job and that the suspension promoted the efficiency of the service because the agency had lost trust in the employee's ability to perform his duties, which involved access to households with children. Furthermore, the employee's presence on the job affected the performance of his co-workers, who were apprehensive of him; see Engdahl v. Dep't. of Navy, 40 M.S.P.R. 660 (1989).

Other types of off-duty criminal misconduct may support an adverse action against the employee where a nexus can be proven. For example, the MSPB found nexus and upheld the imposition of adverse actions, such as demotions and removal, for the criminal conduct of shoplifting and involuntary manslaughter; *see Hawkins v. U.S. Postal Service*, 35

M.S.P.R. 549 (1987) (demotion, not removal, was the appropriate penalty for off-duty shoplifting of an item valued at $16.00); *Taylor v. Dep't. of the Navy,* 35 M.S.P.R. 438 (1987) (removal upheld as appropriate penalty based on an employee's conviction of involuntary manslaughter for unpremeditated strangulation of her son after a five-hour-long religious ceremony intended to exorcise "demons" from the child's body).

Assault

An adverse action will be warranted against an employee who engages in this type of misconduct.

There are some types of misconduct which occur at the workplace where a nexus is obvious. For example, an employee's assault upon his co-workers or supervisors is not permissible. An adverse action will be warranted against an employee who engages in this type of misconduct. In determining the appropriate penalty for a charge of assault, the fact that an employee was provoked by another may act as a mitigating factor. Provocation, however, is just one of the mitigating "Douglas factors" to be considered by the agency and will not necessarily act as a complete defense to the employee's misconduct. (See *Douglas* factors, Chapter 5.)

☑ CASE IN POINT

The MSPB upheld the removal of an employee who slapped another employee, causing injury which necessitated treatment at the agency's health clinic. The employee defended against the removal action by claiming he had been provoked. Though the agency considered the employee's provocation defense, in light of the seriousness of the employee's conduct, his past disciplinary record and other related factors, the MSPB upheld the employee's removal as an appropriate penalty; see Talton v. Dep't. of Army, 36 M.S.P.R. 665 (1988).

Threats

Threats against a supervisor or another employee warrants substantial penalties.

Threatening a supervisor or other employees warrants substantial penalties. There are specific elements to the charge of threatening another person, which must be established by a preponderance of the evidence, before the agency may take an adverse action.

In determining whether a threat warranting an adverse action has been made, a supervisor should consider: 1) the listener's reaction; 2) the listener's real fear of harm; 3) the speaker's intent; 4) any conditional nature of the statements; and 5) the attendant circumstances; *see Metz v. Dep't. of the Treasury,* 780 F.2d 1001 (Fed. Cir. 1986).

☑ CASE IN POINT

During duty hours an employee remarked to his co-worker that if he lost any time "off the clock" he would kick him. The agency proposed the employee's removal based upon this comment. The co-worker against whom the remark was made testified, however, that he did not feel threatened or frightened by the remark, and he did not think that the employee was going to do what he had said. Given the lack of concern exhibited by the co-worker (the listener), it was evident that he did not perceive the comment as a threat, nor did he fear harm. Additionally, the language used by the employee was conditional, i.e., the employee would do something if he was placed "off the clock." Under these circumstances, the charge of threatening a co-worker could not be sustained and would not support the penalty of removal; see Hayslett v. U.S. Postal Service, 38 M.S.P.R. 267 (1988).

Fighting

Supervisors must distinguish threats from angry words. For example, an employee's statement that "you had gall giving me this note concerning my performance knowing all the personal problems I'm having" is not a threat. However, depending on the circumstances, it could be disrespectful behavior for which a lesser discipline may be warranted; *see Carson v. Veterans Administration,* 33 M.S.P.R. 666 (1987).

Falsification

For the violent misconduct of fighting on work time, nexus between the employee's position and the employee's misconduct is presumed. An employee's provocation by another employee, however, may reduce the penalty to be imposed against the employee who initiates a fight on work time. For example, removal will be considered an excessive penalty when one employee provoked another employee into a fight and the provoked employee only suffered a nosebleed and minor bruises; *see Faucher v. U.S. Postal Service,* 41 M.S.P.R. 336 (1989). Supervisors should examine the facts in determining what action to take in response to an employee fight, particularly with respect to the question of whether one of the employees involved in the fight may have been provoked or acting in self-defense.

> A charge of falsification requires evidence that the employee knowingly supplied wrong information with the intent of defrauding the agency.

To sustain a charge of falsification the agency must prove by a preponderance of the evidence that the employee knowingly supplied wrong information with the intention of defrauding the agency; *see Naekel v. Dep't. of Transportation,* 782 F.2d 975 (Fed. Cir. 1986). In other words, a false statement alone is insufficient to establish the charge of falsification. However, an employee's state of mind, such as his intent to deceive, may be inferred from a reckless disregard for the truth or failure to ascertain the truth about the statements made.

☑ CASE IN POINT

An agency removed an employee on the charge of making false statements because the employee stated that: 1) someone was tampering with his food in the cafeteria; 2) a fellow employee broke into his house and stole chocolates; 3) a fellow employee put something in his coffee; 4) his dentist did something to his fillings to allow his conversations to be monitored; 5) his residence was bugged; and 6) he had hired a private investigator to look into it. The agency asserted that the charge of falsification should be sustained and that no "reasonable man" would have believed that any of the statements made by the employee were true. The MSPB held, however, that there was no evidence produced that the employee knew or believed that the statements he made were false. To the contrary, the employee specifically denied that the statements were false. Because the agency failed to prove the requisite intent on the part of the employee, the charge of making false statements was not sustained; see Mooney v. Dep't. of Defense, 44 M.S.P.R. 524 (1990).

An employee's intent to make false statements may be established by circumstantial evidence. Intent may also be inferred when a misrepresentation is made with a reckless disregard for the truth or with a conscious purpose to avoid learning the truth; *see Rigilano v.*

U.S. Postal Service, 41 M.S.P.R. 513 (1989). An employee's defense that he made false statements at the request of his supervisor is not a complete defense to charges of falsification.

☑ CASE IN POINT

An employee who occupied the position of Meat Cutting Foreman at an Air Force base commissary was properly removed for deliberately falsifying inventory reports for the Meat Department, which resulted in losses of more than $19,000, and for requiring subordinates to sign forms indicating they had performed certain meat cutting tests, which they had not performed. The employee defended against his removal by alleging that his supervisor directed him to falsify the inventory reports. The MSPB found that this offense was sufficiently serious to support the removal penalty, despite the employee's defense; see Pitts v. Dep't. of Air Force, 29 M.S.P.R. 108 (1985).

To sustain the charge that an employee falsified government documents, an agency must prove the employee had specific intent to falsify and that false information was given with the intent to deceive or mislead the agency.

☑ CASE IN POINT

An agency suspended an employee for 30 days based upon charges of falsifying promotion applications when the employee indicated on his promotion application that he had received a Bachelor of Arts degree in public administration from an accredited college or university. In fact, the employee had received a Bachelor of Arts degree in public administration from an unaccredited school. The MSPB upheld the 30-day suspension on the basis that the agency had proved the requisite intent for the charge because the employee had acted with reckless disregard for the truth when he knowingly claimed that he had a degree from an accredited institution; see Bryant v. Dep't. of Justice, 39 M.S.P.R. 632 (1989).

An employee's submission of incorrect documents, however, is not necessarily proof of an employee's intent to falsify. A plausible explanation proffered by the employee for submitting incorrect information should be considered in determining the employee's intent. If an agency can demonstrate a specific intent to submit false information with intent to deceive, however, an employee's explanation (e.g., he did not review the documentation which contained the false information before signing it) will not be viewed as sufficient to overcome the agency's showing of specific intent; *see Waddell v. U.S. Postal Service*, 31 M.S.P.R. 80 (1986).

• Falsification of Time and Attendance Cards

To sustain the charge of falsification of time and attendance cards against an employee, the agency must also prove intent. The element of intent can usually be proved by showing that the statement the employee made on the time card was asserted by the employee to be true when the employee knew the statement to be false. The agency must also demonstrate that the employee intended to defraud the agency. Under these circumstances, removal is an appropriate penalty.

> The agency must demonstrate a specific intent on the employee's part to submit false information with the intent to deceive.

A false statement alone is insufficient to establish the charge of falsification.

☑ CASE IN POINT

The Department of the Air Force removed an employee who certified a time and attendance record which reflected that another employee performed active duty for five days when, in fact, the employee performed duty for only three and one-half days. The MSPB upheld the removal, finding that because the employee intended the document to reflect that the other employee worked the hours and days specified, the employee made the false certification with the intent to deceive or mislead the agency. Also, implicit in the finding that the employee falsified the document with the intent to deceive or mislead the agency is the finding that the employee intended to defraud the agency, since these findings were interchangeable. Therefore, the MSPB found that the agency proved the falsification charge by a preponderance of the evidence; see Sherwin v. Dep't. of Air Force, 44 M.S.P.R. 144 (1990).

• Falsification of Travel Documents

The charge of falsification of travel documents may be sustained only if the agency can demonstrate that the employee knowingly supplied wrong information on the travel document and did so with the intention of defrauding the agency. The element of intent in such a case can be negated if the employee demonstrates he sought advice concerning the information contained in his travel claim from a proper source and then followed what turned out later to be wrong advice; *see Listerman v. Dep't. of Justice,* 31 M.S.P.R. 179 (1986). On the other hand, an employee who is familiar with the appropriate procedures for filing travel vouchers and who has had much experience filing claims will be more closely scrutinized; *see Raymond v. Dep't. of Army,* 34 M.S.P.R. 476 (1987).

• False Statements Made During an Investigation

An employee who, in the course of an investigation into his conduct, makes a false statement, cannot be charged with both falsification and with charges related to the underlying misconduct. For example, if during an investigation into whether an employee misused government property, the employee knowingly supplies wrong information about his use, the employee may not be charged both with falsification and with misuse of government property. An agency must either charge the employee with making a false statement, if it believes the elements of falsification are present, or with the misconduct into which it investigated, but not both. *King v. Erickson,* 89 F.3d 1575 (Fed. Cir. 1996). In choosing between a charge of falsification and a charge(s) for the underlying misconduct, an agency should consider the severity of the conduct investigated against the severity of the false statement and charge the employee for the more serious one.

Theft

In charging an employee with theft, the agency must prove all elements of the crime, including intent. Intent in a charge of theft of government property is proven when it is shown that the employee appropriated property for a use inconsistent with the owner's rights and benefits. For example, an employee's use of funds from the office petty cash fund for office supplies, which he gives to his son to use at school, is inconsistent with the intended use of those funds for the government's benefit.

An employee's intent is often established through his state of mind, which is generally proven by circumstantial evidence; *see Messersmith v. General Services Administration,* 9 M.S.P.R. 150 (1981). To sustain the charge of theft, the agency must demonstrate that the employee was in possession of goods not paid for and that the employee had the intent not to pay for these goods; *see Cooper v. U.S. Postal Service,* 42 M.S.P.R. 174 (1989). An employee's off-duty theft may also be actionable. For example, an employee's off-duty shoplifting of goods valued at less than $50 from the military base exchange store warranted the employee's removal; *see Cooper,* above.

A supervisor should consider taking immediate action against an employee who engages in theft. Allowing an employee to continue to work in a position of trust after the supervisor learns of an employee's theft may be raised by the employee as a mitigating factor in favor of a reduced penalty.

☑ CASE IN POINT

An agency removed an employee on the charge that the employee had embezzled money from the government. The agency defended its choice of penalty, in part, with the claim that the employee's embezzlement of government funds was sufficiently serious to lead them to believe that the trust implicit in his job had been violated. The MSPB reduced the employee's penalty to a 90-day suspension, emphasizing that the agency had allowed the employee to continue in his position for a considerable length of time (approximately five months) after learning of the employee's offenses. The agency's conduct, therefore, undermined its assertion that it no longer trusted the employee subsequent to learning of his misconduct; see Goode v. Defense Logistics Agency, 31 M.S.P.R. 446 (1986).

> To sustain a theft charge, the agency must demonstrate the employee was in possession of goods not paid for and that the employee had the intent not to pay for these goods.

Misuse Or Destruction of Government Property

The charge of misuse of government property differs from the charge of theft. An employee may be guilty of misuse of government property, but innocent of theft of government property. For example, an employee who takes a piece of government equipment home, fully intending to return this equipment, may be guilty of misuse of that property. For a charge of misuse of government property the agency is not required to prove intent. Rather, evidence that the employee misused government property alone will be sufficient to sustain the charge; *see Woodard v. Dep't. of the Army,* 18 M.S.P.R 492 (1983).

The charge of misuse of a government vehicle differs from the charge of misuse of government property, because the former charge (misuse of a vehicle) carries with it a minimum statutory penalty of 30 days. (31 U.S.C. 1349(b)) However, a greater penalty can be imposed, if appropriate.

☑ CASE IN POINT

An agency imposed the penalty of removal upon an employee on charges that the employee used a government vehicle for unofficial purposes and that he repeatedly committed recruiting improprieties, violating Army and Recruiting Command regulations. The employee was arrested at approximately 8:00 p.m. and the government vehicle that he

Conflict Of Interest

was driving was impounded by the police. The employee was not in an overtime status at the time of his arrest, and he was not authorized to use the government vehicle. The MSPB upheld the employee's removal, noting that the employee's use of the government vehicle was for other than official purposes, was intentional, and was for personal gain; see Creggett v. Dep't. of Army, 41 M.S.P.R. 584 (1989).

Conflict of interest is a type of misconduct for which an employee may be subject to an adverse action. If an employee expresses concern to a supervisor and requests the advice of a supervisor about the potential for a conflict of interest, the supervisor should refer the employee to the Designated Agency Ethics Official (DAEO). Usually, this person works in the Office of General Counsel. Situations which result in or create the appearance of a conflict of interest may warrant discipline. The appropriate penalty for an employee's violation of the ethical standards that govern the performance of his duties and his ethical conduct is a matter committed largely to the discretion of the agency; *see Miguel v. Dep't. of the Army,* 727 F.2d 1081 (Fed. Cir. 1984).

☑ CASE IN POINT

The Department of the Army removed a GS-12 General Engineer for violating Army regulations when he falsified Daily Construction Records on behalf of an independent contractor with whom he had become closely associated. Such conduct constituted a breach of the employee's responsibility to administer contracts fairly and created a clear conflict of interest because it is the duty of the General Engineer impartially to supervise independent contractors. The penalty of removal was upheld by the MSPB, which noted that the conflict of interest alone was serious enough to warrant removal; see Dickinson v. Dep't. of the Army, 32 M.S.P.R. 372 (1987).

The fact that an employee was not warned that his conduct violated the standards of conduct does not necessarily excuse the employee's misconduct. Employees are presumed to be familiar with rules and governing laws; *see Faitel v. Veterans Administration,* 26 M.S.P.R. 465 (1985).

Ethical Violations

Violation of the new ethics regulations can serve as the basis for a misconduct adverse action.

For the first time, the Office of Government Ethics (OGE) has issued a set of comprehensive federal employment ethics. The regulations took effect February 3, 1993. The guidelines for employees of the Executive Branch are located at 5 C.F.R. Part 2635 and replace not only the rules formerly located at Part 2635, but also supersede all rules previously in place at individual agencies. The new rules cover conduct involving the giving and receiving of gifts, conflicting financial interests, impartiality in performing duties, seeking post-government employment, misuse of an official government position, and outside activities. Any alleged violation of the new ethics regulations can serve as the basis for a misconduct adverse action against a federal employee. These ethics rules are discussed in detail in Chapter 20. Individual agencies may issue supplemental rules, but those must not conflict with the OGE rules and may not be implemented until OGE has reviewed and approved them.

Sexual Harassment And Other Discriminatory Acts

Failure to effectively deal with instances of sexual harassment can itself lead to a charge of sexual harassment.

• **Discriminatory Acts**

Pursuant to Title VII of the Civil Rights Act of 1964, discrimination in the workplace on the basis of race, color, religion, national origin, or sex is prohibited. Discrimination on the basis of age or physical or mental handicap is also prohibited by the Age Discrimination in Employment Act, (ADEA) and the Rehabilitation Act, respectively. These laws are applicable to the federal government and regulations have been issued by the Equal Employment Opportunity Commission (EEOC). (See Chapter 14 for a more detailed discussion.) Employees who engage in unlawful discrimination may be disciplined.

☑ CASE IN POINT

An employee was debarred from federal service for a period of five years as a penalty for engaging in religious discrimination against another employee in the office. More specifically, the employee made derogatory religious comments and "slurs" about another employee over a two-year period. The employee also arranged a mock satire of the crucifixion, focusing attention on the only Jewish employee in the office by requiring that employee to play the lead role of Jesus. The MSPB upheld the penalty of debarment in this case, based in part on the employee's flagrant religious discrimination; see Special Counsel v. Zimmerman, 36 M.S.P.R. 274 (1988).

• **Sexual Harassment**

Sexual harassment is defined generally as unwelcome sexual advances, requests for sexual favors, and other verbal or physical conduct of a sexual nature when:

1) submission to such conduct is a term or condition of employment;

2) submission to or rejection of such conduct is used as a basis for decisions affecting an individual's employment; or

3) such conduct has the purpose or effect of interfering with an individual's performance or creating an intimidating, hostile or offensive working environment. (29 C.F.R. 1604.11.)

Sexual harassment is usually characterized as one of two types:

1) *quid pro quo* harassment, or

2) harassment in the form of creating an intimidating, hostile or offensive work environment.

An employee who has sexually harassed a subordinate or a co-worker should be disciplined. The failure to effectively deal with instances of sexual harassment can itself lead to a charge of sexual harassment. (See Chapter 15 for a more detailed discussion of sexual harassment.)

Drug Charges

The illegal use of drugs is a serious offense and should be treated as such by the agency. The purchase and/or sale of drugs on the worksite may warrant the penalty of removal. This type of conduct permits the inference of untrustworthiness on the employee's part. The MSPB has upheld the penalty of removal for charges related to the sale of drugs, such as cocaine, on the worksite; *see Best v. U.S. Postal Service,* 41 M.S.P.R. 124 (1989). Furthermore, the mere possession of drugs on the worksite may warrant removal.

On the other hand, the MSPB found the penalty of removal for an employee's unauthorized possession of marijuana on agency premises to be too severe a penalty where the misconduct was the employee's first disciplinary offense and the employee had more than 23 years of frequently exemplary service with no prior disciplinary record. Instead, a 60-day suspension was imposed; *see Tierney v. Dep't. of Navy,* 44 M.S.P.R. 153 (1990).

An employee who is subjected to disciplinary action based on drug-related charges may claim as a defense that he has an addiction to drugs, which caused his misconduct. Under certain circumstances, a drug addiction may be considered a handicap for which accommodation by the agency is warranted. (See discussion in Chapter 17.) An employee's conviction on drug charges, however, may warrant severe discipline against the employee.

☑ CASE IN POINT

An agency removed an employee on the ground that he was convicted on felony charges of conspiracy to possess and distribute cocaine. The employee pleaded guilty to the charges and received a fine and suspended prison sentence.

The MSPB upheld the employee's removal on the charge of criminal and dishonest conduct unbecoming a federal employee. The employee worked without direct supervision and was responsible for more than $100 million worth of equipment; see Rusnack v. Dep't. of Commerce, 36 M.S.P.R. 551 (1988).

Alcohol-Related Charges

Both offenses of possession of alcohol while on duty and alcohol-related misconduct while off-duty may warrant penalties as serious as removal. Until recently, a supervisor who was considering an adverse action against an employee for engaging in alcohol-related misconduct, was required to consider whether the employee would raise the defense of handicap based on alcoholism and if the employee raised such a defense, an agency was required to offer the employee a "firm choice" between treatment and discipline. Due to recent changes to the Rehabilitation Act, if the employee is alcohol-dependent and the misconduct was caused by the handicap (e.g., falling asleep at work because he is an alcoholic who got drunk on duty) the agency is no longer required to accommodate the employee with a "firm choice" prior to taking disciplinary action against him; *see Kimble v. Dep't of Navy,* 70 M.S.P.R. 617, 622 (1996). While the "firm choice" accommodations are no longer required, federal agencies may offer such accommodations at their discretion. (See discussion of alcoholic employees in Chapter 17.)

If the employee presents no defense of handicap discrimination, however, dealing with an adverse action based on alcohol-related charges should be handled like any other type of misconduct. For example, an employee may be appropriately removed for possession of alcohol while on duty and for other minor absences from the duty station without authorization; *see Lockett v. U.S. Marine Corps,* 43 M.S.P.R. 108 (1990). Similarly, off-duty alcohol related misconduct may warrant removal.

☑ CASE IN POINT

An agency removed an employee, who, while driving his government vehicle in the wrong lane on an interstate highway, collided with an oncoming car, killing a two-year-old child.

At the scene of the accident the employee's blood alcohol content test revealed that his blood alcohol level was 2.07 percent, well above that state's legal limit of .10 percent. The employee raised as a defense handicap discrimination based on alcoholism. The MSPB upheld the agency's removal of the employee, noting that the employee's misconduct was disqualifying, egregious misconduct. The MSPB found that engaging in such egregious misconduct disqualified the employee from raising the handicap defense of alcoholism. Furthermore, the agency was responsible for enforcing and administering firearms, arson and explosive laws, in addition to laws governing the production, use and distribution of alcohol and tobacco products. The employee, a Special Agent, carried a gun, drove a government vehicle, and had arrest authority. On these facts, the MSPB found that the employee's misconduct struck at the core of the agency's mission and the employee's duties as a law enforcement officer; see Wilber v. Dep't. of Treasury, 42 M.S.P.R. 582 (1989).

> An agency is no longer required to accommodate an alcohol-dependent employee with a "firm choice" prior to taking disciplinary action against him.

Nepotism

Nepotism is favoritism shown to a relative, such as appointing a relative to a job on the basis of relationship. Nepotism in the federal government is specifically prohibited by the law. (5 U.S.C. 3110) Section 3110 provides that a public official may not appoint, employ, promote, advance, or advocate for appointment, employment, promotion, or advancement, in or to a civilian position in the agency in which the official is serving or over which he exercises jurisdiction or control, any individual who is a relative of the public official. An adverse action may be initiated against an employee who engages in nepotism.

Improper Favoritism Personnel Actions

Supervisors or managers who grant unauthorized favors to enhance someone's prospect for promotion or appointment may be disciplined for committing a prohibited personnel practice. (5 U.S.C. 2302 (b)(6))

This includes granting temporary appointment to someone who is ineligible for a permanent appointment so that the person becomes eligible for a permanent job.

Other Types Of Conduct Warranting Adverse Action

• Security

Clearance

Revocation

• Medical

Certification

• Refusing

Geographic

Reassignment

• Debts

☑ **CASE IN POINT**

Edward directed that a subordinate, Diane, prepare a written justification for the temporary appointment of his son to a federal job over which he had indirect control. The written justification was then presented to the State Executive Director for approval. The agency suspended Edward and reassigned him, based on the charge of nepotism and other misconduct. The MSPB upheld the charges against Edward and affirmed the agency's choice of penalty; see Welch v. Dep't. of Agriculture, 37 M.S.P.R. 18 (1988).

Not all conduct warranting adverse action can be labeled as misconduct. For example, an employee's failure to maintain a certification or condition necessary to perform his job may be cause to subject the employee to adverse action.

• Security Clearance Revocation

If the job requires maintenance of a security clearance and the clearance is revoked, the agency may take adverse action against the employee. Under current law, the decision to revoke a security clearance rests entirely with an agency and may not be reviewed or modified by the MSPB or the courts.

☑ **CASE IN POINT**

The indefinite suspension of an employee is often used in the interim period between the time an employee is suspected of committing a crime and a final disposition in the criminal investigation or prosecution; see Jones v. Dep't. of Navy, 48 M.S.P.R. 680 (1991), modified by, 51 M.S.P.R. 607, aff'd, 978 F.2d 1223 (Fed. Cir. 1992). In the Jones case, two employees' security clearances were suspended pending the agency's investigation of cocaine use and possession. Since without their security clearances the employees could not perform their duties, they were placed in leave without pay status and were suspended indefinitely. The MSPB held that the agency could invoke an indefinite suspension with "reasonable cause" that a crime has been committed for which imprisonment may be imposed, and that an indefinite suspension does not have to be reversed at a later date if it was proper when effected.

The decision in *Jones* significantly expands the holdings of prior decisions, in which employees actually had been indicted and prosecuted prior to being suspended indefinitely without pay pending the outcome of the employees' security clearances, necessary for their work. The use of an indefinite suspension was recently expanded to an employee whose access to classified information was suspended pending an investigation into whether the employee suffered from a medical condition which disqualified him from holding a security clearance; *see O.P.M. v. Alston,* 75 F.3d 657 (Fed. Cir. 1996). The decision in *Alston* takes the *Jones* case one-step further as a precedent for effecting an indefinite suspension against employees whose eligibility for security clearances is under investigation for reasons completely unrelated to any criminal process.

A remarkable feature of security clearance cases, and what makes *Jones* and *Alston* a powerful tool for agencies, is the Supreme Court's position that an agency decision to suspend a security clearance indefinitely is essentially non-reviewable; *see Dep't. of Navy v. Egan,* 484 U.S. 518 (1988) (holding that the MSPB lacks the authority to review the underlying reasons for the denial of a security clearance).

• Medical Certification

An adverse action may also appropriately be taken against an employee for the loss of a medical certification. There are certain positions in the government which require employees to meet specific medical standards and to be certified upon initial employment and maintain that same medical certification in order to be retained in their positions. Like a security clearance revocation, a failure to maintain the medical certification may result in the employee's removal.

☑ CASE IN POINT

The Federal Aviation Administration requires that air traffic controllers meet specific medical standards, be certified upon initial employment, and maintain that same medical certification in order to retain their positions. An agency employee was properly removed after the employee's medical certification was withdrawn by the agency, based on evidence showing the employee had twice, during the course of his recent employment, been admitted to the hospital because of a diagnosed psychiatric disorder. The agency's regulations provided that an established medical history or clinical diagnosis of a psychiatric disorder or of a mental, neurotic or personality disorder was disqualifying. Also, the employee had been hospitalized for a psychiatric disorder prior to securing federal employment, yet the employee failed to indicate this fact on his application for a medical certification; see Cosby v. Federal Aviation Administration, 30 M.S.P.R. 16 (1986).

If the agency wishes to remove an employee based on loss of a medical certification, the agency must demonstrate by a preponderance of the evidence the basis for the revocation of the medical certification and that the penalty is appropriate after considering all relevant *Douglas* factors. (See discussion of the *Douglas* factors and appropriate penalties in Chapter 5.)

Under some circumstances, an employee's physical inability to perform the duties of the position may require the agency to take an adverse action.

☑ CASE IN POINT

An agency removed an employee who occupied the position of Painting Helper based on the employee's physical inability to perform the duties of his position. After the employee suffered an epileptic seizure and took a fitness for duty examination, the agency physician restricted the employee from climbing ladders or working around machinery. The employee could, therefore, no longer perform the essential duties of the Painting Helper position. The MSPB upheld the employee's removal, finding that the employee was not a "qualified handicapped employee" because he could not perform the essential duties of his position, even with reasonable accommodation, and because he did not have the experience or physical qualification requirements for any other position to which he could have been assigned; see Miss v. Dep't. of Air Force, 34 M.S.P.R. 8 (1987).

Like a security clearance revocation, failure to maintain medical certification may result in the employee's removal.

If all criteria are demonstrated by the agency for reassignment of an employee, the employee's failure to accept the reassignment and appear for duty may form the basis for adverse action.

• **Refusing Geographic Reassignment**

A supervisor may also initiate an adverse action against an employee who refuses to accept a reassignment. In order to sustain this adverse action, the agency must demonstrate that there was a legitimate management reason for the reassignment, that the employee had adequate notice of the reassignment, and that the employee refused to accept the reassignment. If these criteria are demonstrated by the agency, the employee's failure to accept the reassignment and to appear for duty at the new duty station may form the basis for adverse action, up to and including removal; *see Taylor v. Dep't. of Health and Human Services,* 40 M.S.P.R. 106 (1989).

• **Debts**

Disciplinary action may also be initiated against an employee for failure to pay just debts. (*See* 5 C.F.R. 2635.809) Ordinarily, a just debt is one that is reduced to judgment or which is acknowledged by the employee. The failure to pay one's just debts is often an issue that arises in the course of a security clearance investigation. The issue also arises if the employee's debts are incurred through use of a government credit card and the employee occupies a position involving fiduciary responsibility, in which case the employee is considered to have engaged in serious misconduct for which a substantial penalty can be imposed. Otherwise, failure to pay just debts is an offense most often handled by counseling or a reprimand, unless the debt is to the government or is for failure to pay child support. (*See* 5 C.F.R. Part 581) Debts to the government and those for child support may subject the employee's wages to garnishment if authorized by a court of appropriate jurisdiction. As of February 1994, other debts which are reduced to a judgment may also be subject to garnishment. (*See* 5 C.F.R. Part 582)

☑ CASE IN POINT

Faye was removed from her position as Travel Assistant based on the charge of failure to pay her just debts in a proper and timely manner and on other charges of misconduct related to falsification and refusal to answer appropriate questions regarding her social security number and her indebtedness. Faye had failed to pay, for 15 months, the balance on her government-issued Diners Club credit card, even though she had been reimbursed by the agency. In light of Faye's duties as a Travel Assistant, wherein she advised other employees about the policy that Diners Club bills must be paid before the next billing cycle, and the fiduciary responsibilities of the position, the MSPB upheld the penalty of removal; see Dorrough v. Dep't. of Commerce, 41 M.S.P.R. 87 (1989).

Conclusion

Remember, not all misconduct fits into a category.

Dealing with an employee who engages in misconduct is part of a supervisor's inherent responsibility. Hopefully, the review of the various types of misconduct discussed in this chapter will make defining, analyzing and choosing the appropriate penalty for discipline a less formidable task for the supervisor. Remember, however, that not all misconduct necessarily fits into a category. An appropriate disciplinary action against an employee who engages in misconduct must only meet the standard that the discipline promotes the efficiency of the service.

Choosing Appropriate Discipline

Choosing Appropriate Discipline

After a supervisor establishes that misconduct has occurred and that the misconduct has a relationship to the employee's job (see Chapters 2 and 3), the next step is to choose an appropriate penalty. This can be one of the more difficult decisions a federal supervisor is required to make. The Merit Systems Protection Board (MSPB) has prescribed the *Douglas* factors (see facing page) in choosing an appropriate penalty, and some agencies also have their own guidelines, called a table of penalties, to assist supervisors. Careful consideration of the following information before deciding on a penalty will help assure that any reviewer affirms the penalty chosen by agency management.

Progressive Discipline And Agency Table Of Penalties

The theory of progressive discipline is usually built into the agency table of penalties.

In choosing an appropriate penalty, supervisors should follow the practice of progressive discipline. Progressive discipline means that the least serious penalty which will correct the problem should be imposed for a first offense and that more serious forms of discipline can be imposed for repeated offenses of misconduct. For example, removal would be considered too serious a penalty to impose against a long-term employee with no prior history of misconduct who, on only one occasion, is 30 minutes tardy with an inadequate explanation. Counseling or an oral admonishment would be a more appropriate penalty. If the employee's tardiness is repeated, however, or if the employee later engages in a different type of misconduct, the discipline that could reasonably be imposed against the employee will increase and become more serious. An employee's second offense of tardiness could warrant a written reprimand or a short suspension. Repeated tardiness after previous discipline may warrant a very serious penalty, such as a long suspension or even removal.

Progressive discipline is used most often to determine the appropriate penalty for minor misconduct. For serious offenses, such as repeated or extensive absence without leave (AWOL), criminal charges, or filing false travel claims, more severe discipline could be warranted even for a first offense.

To assist supervisors in determining the appropriate penalty, many agencies have implemented a table of penalties. The theory of progressive discipline is usually built into the table. A typical table of penalties will list the type of offense and the types of discipline which would be appropriate. The types of discipline correspond with whether the discipline is for a first, second, or third offense. Supervisors should consult with their personnel office to determine if a table of penalties exists. If the agency has a table of penalties and fails to follow it, the employee may assert this failure as a defense in challenging the discipline chosen by the supervisor; *see Goode v. Defense Logistics Agency,* 45 M.S.P.R. 671 (1990). If an agency has no table of penalties, a supervisor has more discretion in choosing an appropriate penalty.

The "Douglas" Factors

The MSPB has developed a set of criteria to be considered by federal managers when deciding what penalty to impose for an employee's misconduct. These factors were set forth by the MSPB in the precedent setting case of *Douglas v. Veterans Administration,* 5 M.S.P.R. 280 (1981). These factors guide the selection of an appropriate penalty in misconduct cases involving employees at all levels of federal service, including the Senior Executive Service.

In *Douglas,* the employee was removed from his agency for being absent without leave for 30 minutes, for being away from his assigned duty station without permission, and for selling his employment services to a physically handicapped employee.

In selecting the penalty of removal, the agency considered four past disciplinary actions: a two-year-old admonishment for eight hours of AWOL; a two-year-old reprimand for failure to report for duty and four hours of AWOL; a two-year-old five-day suspension for a 45-minute period of AWOL; and, a six-month-old 20-day suspension for another period of AWOL. The employee in *Douglas* argued that the agency's penalty of removal was too severe. The penalty of removal was accepted by the MSPB. However, in evaluating the case and the penalty, the MSPB established the criteria federal managers are to consider in determining the appropriate penalty. These criteria, commonly known as the "Douglas" factors, are as follows:

- The nature and seriousness of the offense, and its relation to the employee's duties, position, and responsibilities, including whether the offense was intentional, technical or inadvertent, or was committed maliciously or for gain, or was frequently repeated;

- The employee's job level and type of employment, including supervisory, or fiduciary role, contacts with the public, and prominence of the position;

- The employee's past disciplinary record;

- The employee's past work record, including length of service, performance on the job, ability to get along with fellow workers, and dependability;

- The effect of the offense upon the employee's ability to perform at a satisfactory level and its effect upon supervisors' confidence in the employee's ability to perform assigned duties;

- Consistency of the penalty with those imposed upon other employees for the same or similar offenses;

- Consistency of the penalty with any applicable agency table of penalties;

- The notoriety of the offense or its impact upon the reputation of the agency;

- The clarity with which the employee was on notice of any rules that were violated in committing the offense, or had been warned about the conduct in question;

- Potential for the employee's rehabilitation;

> The "Douglas" Factors guide the selection of an appropriate penalty in misconduct cases involving employees at all levels of federal service.

Failure to properly and fully consider the Douglas factors will create problems if a disciplinary action is challenged.

- Mitigating circumstances surrounding the offense such as unusual job tensions, personality problems, mental impairment, harassment, or bad faith, malice or provocation on the part of others involved in the matter; and,

- The adequacy and effectiveness of alternative sanctions to deter such conduct in the future by the employee or others.

The importance of considering the *Douglas* factors in determining an appropriate penalty cannot be overstated. Should an employee challenge a manager's choice of penalty at the MSPB, the manager will be successful in defending his or her selection only if the manager considered the relevant *Douglas* factors in determining the penalty and was reasonable in the selection of a penalty.

A rational articulation of the reasons why the penalty was chosen and how the *Douglas* factors related to the decision will virtually guarantee affirmance of the penalty by the MSPB or an arbitrator in cases where the MSPB sustains all the charges brought against the employee. On the other hand, failure to properly and fully consider the *Douglas* factors will create problems if a disciplinary action is challenged. The MSPB will conduct its own *Douglas* factor evaluation, and in cases where the MSPB sustains all the charges, it will only approve the maximum reasonable penalty appropriate for the offense as determined by the MSPB's administrative judge hearing the case.

Until recently, the MSPB also applied the "maximum reasonable penalty" standard of review to cases where it did not sustain all of the charges. The Board has decided that the same standard for reviewing an agency's penalty determination, regardless of whether all of the charges were sustained by the Board, ignored the distinction between cases where it sustained all the charges and those where it did not. In the former, the agency has made a penalty determination based solely on the sustained charges which the Board found it could measure against a reasonableness standard and correct the agency determination when it exceeds the bounds of reasonableness. In the latter situation, where the MSPB does not sustain all the charges, it has concluded that the basis for the agency imposed penalty no longer exists. Thus, "there is no clear and measurable agency determination which can be corrected if it exceeds the parameters of reasonableness;" *White v. U.S. Postal Service,* 1996 WL 593867 (M.S.P.B.). The Board, therefore, concluded that agency penalty determinations were to be given no deference in employee appeals of adverse actions, where it does not sustain all the charges. In these appeals, the MSPB will independently balance the relevant *Douglas* factors and select a "reasonable" penalty. Id.

A supervisor need not consider all of the *Douglas* factors in each case. For example, the *Douglas* factor that requires consideration of the consistency of the chosen penalty with the applicable agency table of penalties would be irrelevant if the agency had no table of penalties. A more detailed explanation of each separate *Douglas* factor is provided on the following page.

Douglas Factors Quick Reference

No. 1   Nature and seriousness of the offense.

No. 2   Employee's job level and type of employment.

No. 3   Employee's past disciplinary record.

No. 4   Employee's past work record.

No. 5   Effect of the offense upon the employee's ability to perform at a satisfactory level.

No. 6   Consistency with similarly-situated employees.

No. 7   Consistency with table of penalties.

No. 8   Notoriety of the offense.

No. 9   Clarity with which employee is on notice of any rule violated by misconduct.

No. 10   Potential for the employee's rehabilitation.

No. 11   Other mitigating circumstances.

No. 12   Adequacy of alternative sanctions to deter future conduct.

Douglas Factors Summary

Douglas Factor No. 1 - The Nature and Seriousness of the Offense

A logical factor to consider in choosing discipline against an employee is the nature and seriousness of the employee's misconduct. Other related aspects are the relationship of the misconduct to the employee's duties, position and responsibilities; whether the offense was intentional or inadvertent; and, whether the offense was committed maliciously, for gain, or was frequently repeated.

For example, the misconduct of falsification of time and attendance records is universally recognized as an extremely serious offense which directly affects the employer-employee relationship and will be found to support a severe penalty, even for an employee who has many years of service and no prior disciplinary record. Furthermore, the intentional nature of the falsification will enhance the seriousness of the charge. If an employee repeatedly and knowingly falsified his time and attendance records to indicate that the employee was at work when he was not, even a previous good work record, long tenure, and absence of a record of prior discipline would not prevent the agency from imposing a severe penalty, such as demotion or removal.

Whether the employee's misconduct was for personal gain and intentional is also a factor considered regarding the seriousness of the charge. For example, an employee's intentional use of a government vehicle for his personal purposes contributes to the seriousness of the offense of misuse of a government vehicle. A lengthy suspension or removal, depending upon consideration of the other relevant *Douglas* factors, may be warranted.

Furthermore, in considering the appropriate penalty for theft, the value of the item taken should be considered in assessing the seriousness of the misconduct.

☑ CASE IN POINT

An employee who shoplifted a kitchen knife worth $3.59 at a local grocery store may be subject to discipline for violation of the agency's code of ethical conduct. Yet, the de minimis value of the item taken, along with consideration of the other Douglas factors, such as the employee's length of government service, his good work record, and the absence of any recent disciplinary actions, rendered the penalty of removal too severe. Mitigation of the penalty to a 30-day suspension was considered appropriate under the circumstances; see Mallery v. U.S. Postal Service, 41 M.S.P.R. 288 (1989).

Douglas Factor No. 2 - Employee's Job Level and Type of Employment

A supervisor should also consider the employee's job level, type of employment, and the prominence of the employee's position. If the employee who commits misconduct is a supervisor or has a fiduciary role where truthfulness, trustworthiness and reliability are required in the position, then these aspects must be factored into the decision. Depending on the other circumstances of the case, the penalty of removal or reduction in grade to a non-supervisory position may be the appropriate penalty.

☑ CASE IN POINT

The U.S. Postal Service proposed the removal of one of its supervisors who engaged in the misconduct of improperly disposing of mail.

The supervisor instructed a postal custodian to discard a cart filled with second-class and bulk business mail that should have been processed for address correction prior to being discarded. On appeal to the MSPB, the Board noted the seriousness of the employee's offense, particularly because the employee occupied a supervisory position and was therefore held to a higher standard of care in his work performance. However, the employee had approximately seven years of service with the agency, three years of military service, and his work performance had been previously satisfactory with no prior disciplinary record. The MSPB characterized the misconduct as a single instance of poor judgment and reduced the penalty to demotion to a non-supervisory position, rather than removal. The Board reasoned that this penalty recognized the seriousness of the employee's misconduct and yet was severe enough to ensure that the employee would refrain from such misconduct in the future. It also put other employees on notice that such conduct will not be tolerated; see Bonacchi v. U.S. Postal Service, 40 M.S.P.R. 364 (1989).

In proposing an appropriate penalty, the supervisor should consider the employee's job level, type of employment and prominence of the employee's position.

Douglas Factor No. 3 - Employee's Past Disciplinary Record

Ordinarily, a supervisor may consider a prior disciplinary action as an aggravating factor justifying the imposition of a more severe penalty. The previous discipline may be considered in determining the appropriate penalty for the most recent offense if at the time of the prior action the employee was: 1) informed of the action in writing; 2) given the opportunity to grieve or appeal the action to a higher authority, and 3) the action was made a matter of record.

If these criteria are met, the employee cannot re-argue the merits of the prior discipline in the appeal of the current disciplinary action; *see Ballew v. Dep't of the Army,* 36 M.S.P.R. 400 (1988).

Remember that all three of the above criteria must be met before a supervisor is permitted to consider prior disciplinary action. For example, if a supervisor relies upon a previous suspension, which the employee was not told he could have appealed or grieved, this failure would prevent the supervisor from considering the prior disciplinary action. However, if the employee has a grievance pending on a prior disciplinary action, a supervisor may properly consider the prior discipline to enhance the penalty for the most recent misconduct; *see Jeffers v. Veterans Administration,* 40 M.S.P.R. 567 (1989).

If the supervisor intends to rely upon prior disciplinary actions to enhance the penalty to be imposed for the current misconduct, the supervisor should state this in the notice to the employee proposing the current disciplinary action. If the employee's prior disciplinary record is not referred to in both the proposed disciplinary action notice and the agency's final decision, it may not be relied upon by the agency in choosing the appropriate penalty. Also, it will not be relied upon by the administrative judge in an appeal to the MSPB.

> If the supervisor intends to rely upon prior disciplinary action to enhance the penalty for the current misconduct, he should state this in the notice to the employee.

☑ CASE IN POINT

In a disciplinary action at the U.S. Postal Service, the agency relied upon an employee's two previous suspensions and a letter of warning. These were not referred to in either the notice to the employee proposing his removal or the notice of decision to the employee imposing the penalty of removal. On appeal, the administrative judge also relied upon the previous disciplinary record of the employee in determining the appropriateness of the penalty.

The MSPB found that this consideration by the agency and the administrative judge was improper; see Reed v. U.S. Postal Service, 33 M.S.P.R. 9 (1987).

Douglas Factor No. 4 - Employee's Past Work Record

The length of an employee's government service and the employee's performance on the job are appropriate factors to consider in assessing an appropriate penalty. For example, although the penalty of removal may be considered an appropriate penalty for the severe misconduct of falsification of time and attendance records, an employee's 30-year-record of excellent service and dependability may mitigate this penalty to a less severe form of discipline, such as a lengthy suspension or demotion.

☑ CASE IN POINT

An employee who managed a golf pro shop at an Air Force base used a personal account with a golf equipment vendor to benefit his friends in a manner that denied the pro shop the opportunity to profit from sales to his friends. The employee had 40 years of unblemished federal service at the time of the disciplinary action against him. The employee was a manager who had received excellent prior performance ratings, as well as numerous testimonials from superiors, co-workers and customers. In light of the employee's lengthy government service and his excellent performance on the job, the penalty of removal was mitigated to a 60-day suspension; see DiMaggio v. Dep't. of Air Force, 28 M.S.P.R. 321 (1985).

Douglas Factor No. 5 - Effect of Offense Upon Employee's Ability to Perform at a Satisfactory Level

Some forms of misconduct may have a negative effect upon the supervisor's confidence in the employee's ability to perform.

Depending upon the type of position the employee holds, some forms of misconduct may have a negative effect upon the employee's continued ability to perform at a satisfactory level in the position. Other misconduct may have a negative effect upon the supervisor's confidence in the employee's ability to perform. For example, a federal supervisor with procurement responsibilities must be relied upon and trusted by his superiors in order for them to feel confident about the employee's ability to carry out the sensitive nature of his duties. An employee's breach of that trust and confidence through misconduct will diminish the superior's confidence in the employee. These circumstances may warrant an enhanced penalty, such as demotion from a supervisory position, or assignment to a position requiring less responsibility or a reduced degree of trust.

Douglas Factor No. 6 - Consistency of the Penalty with Those Imposed Upon Other Employees for the Same or Similar Offense

In determining the appropriateness of a penalty, supervisors should consider penalties imposed upon similarly-situated employees for similar offenses. Employees are likely to raise as a defense to a chosen penalty the claim that they were treated unfairly, if similarly-situated employees who committed similar misconduct received less severe penalties.

An essential element to countering an employee's claim of such "disparate treatment" is a showing that the charges and the circumstances surrounding the charged behavior are substantially different from those of the other employees who were treated more favorably.

☑ CASE IN POINT

An Air Traffic Control Specialist was removed from his position for failure to complete the required Air Traffic Control Specialist training program. The employee challenged his removal and alleged that the agency continued to employ several other persons who did not successfully complete the Air Traffic Controller training. However, the agency was able to prove that the other employees who were retained were in substantially different positions and were not in jobs similar to that of the affected employee. The employee's defense of disparate treatment was therefore rejected by the MSPB; see Grassell v. Dep't. of Transportation, 40 M.S.P.R. 554 (1989).

In determining whether charges and circumstances surrounding the misconduct are substantially similar, a supervisor should review the actual charge against the employee and the chosen discipline and consider whether the circumstances surrounding that behavior are substantially similar to those of other cases where less severe forms of discipline have been imposed. Comparison should be made only among employees who occupy relatively similar positions of trust and responsibility. Furthermore, the employee claiming disparate treatment may only compare himself to other employees in the same organizational unit; *see Taylor v. Dep't. of Navy*, 35 M.S.P.R. 438 (1987).

Military personnel cannot be compared to civilian employees for purposes of establishing disparate treatment; *see King v. Dep't. of the Army*, 16 M.S.P.R. 121 (1983), *aff'd*, 732 F.2d 168 (Fed. Cir. 1984).

It should be noted that the similarity of the penalty with those imposed upon other similarly-situated employees is only one of the 12 Douglas factors to be considered in determining an appropriate penalty. Even where similar misconduct is committed by two similarly-situated employees, factors such as the employee's work record, job level, disciplinary record, length of government service, and the employee's potential for rehabilitation must still be considered and could justify the imposition of a different penalty.

Douglas Factor No. 7 - Consistency of the Penalty with Agency Table of Penalties

As discussed earlier, to assist supervisors in determining an appropriate penalty some agencies implement their own table of penalties. If the agency has a table of penalties, the supervisor should consult it in connection with choosing the appropriate discipline. Any deviation from the table of penalties must be supported by a strong, rational justification. If the agency does not have a currently implemented table of penalties, supervisors need not be concerned with this *Douglas* factor.

> If an agency has a table of penalties, any deviation from the table must be supported by a strong, rational justification.

Douglas Factor No. 8 - Notoriety of the Offense

Misconduct which causes embarrassment to the agency and/or creates a public scandal may result in the imposition of a more severe penalty. For example, an employee who submits false information in response to a congressional inquiry, which then results in public embarrassment to the agency and damage to its reputation, may be subject to a more severe penalty. However, if the misconduct is not widely known, this fact could be used as a mitigating factor in the employee's favor.

Douglas Factor No. 9 - Clarity with Which Employee is on Notice of Any Rule Violated by the Misconduct

In responding to a notice of proposed disciplinary action, an employee may raise as a defense his lack of knowledge of the impropriety of the misconduct or the existence of the rule with which he is charged as having violated. Depending upon the circumstances, this could be an effective defense. An employee's violation of a little-known and obscure agency policy would be viewed less harshly than an employee's violation of an agency regulation about which he was previously warned and of which he was clearly on notice. However, while this defense may be used to mitigate a penalty under *Douglas,* it is generally not a good defense to the charges themselves, since employees are presumed to know the requirements of the law and their agency's rules of conduct.

Douglas Factor No. 10 - Potential for the Employee's Rehabilitation

An employee's capacity for rehabilitation may be considered in imposing discipline. For example, an employee who responds to a notice of proposed disciplinary action claiming his conduct was completely appropriate, or who blames his misconduct on others, demonstrates the employee's failure to accept responsibility for his conduct, and therefore shows he has a decreased potential for rehabilitation. On the other hand, an employee who accepts responsibility for his actions and takes subsequent measures to correct his conduct and to assure his supervisors and others that the conduct will not be repeated, shows more potential for rehabilitation, thus warranting a less severe penalty.

Douglas Factor No. 11- Other Mitigating Circumstances

Other mitigating circumstances surrounding the employee's conduct, such as unusual job tensions, personal problems, mental impairment, harassment, bad faith, malice or provocation on the part of others involved in the matter, should be considered. For example, an employee knows that certain government equipment must be kept in the government office, but with a deadline fast approaching to complete the briefing paper for senior management, the employee uses poor judgment one evening and takes the government equipment home with him so that he may work on the project at his house. The unusual job

> A less severe penalty may be warranted if the employee accepts responsibility for his actions and shows potential for rehabilitation.

tensions which motivated the employee to take the government property home could act as a mitigating factor in determining the appropriate penalty for the employee's misconduct; *cf. Davis v. Department of Army*, 33 M.S.P.R. 223 (1987).

Another situation where it might be appropriate to consider other mitigating circumstances is where an employee rashly uses harsh words toward his supervisor. A mitigating circumstance to a charge of disrespectful conduct could be the supervisor's bad faith in taunting the employee, based on the employee having "blown the whistle" on the supervisor several weeks beforehand for engaging in illegal activities. In this situation, the supervisor's bad faith and provocation of the employee could be a mitigating circumstance. Also, one employee's constant harassment of another employee could be considered provocation if the victimized employee subsequently had a fight with the harassing employee; *see Wilburn v. U.S. Postal Service*, 28 M.S.P.R. 524 (1985).

☑ CASE IN POINT

Harry was removed from the Postal Service for starting a fight with another employee, Jim. The incident began after Jim sent a large metal cart filled with mail speeding through swinging doors toward Harry. Harry barely escaped being struck by jumping out of the way. When Harry confronted Jim about his conduct, Jim taunted Harry by yelling "What's wrong, too fast for you?" A scuffle then ensued, wherein Jim suffered bruises and a nosebleed. Jim's provocation in this case was treated as a mitigating factor, and Harry's penalty of removal was reduced to a 60-day suspension; see Faucher v. U.S. Postal Service, 41 M.S.P.R. 336 (1989).

Douglas Factor No. 12 - Adequacy of Alternative Sanctions to Deter Conduct in the Future

There are some instances, particularly for minor types of misconduct, where alternative sanctions may serve as a deterrent to the employee not to repeat the same misconduct in the future. For example, for disruptive conduct in the workplace, the employee's public apology to the harmed party and the imposition of a letter of caution could serve as a sufficient deterrent to the employee repeating the same type of misconduct.

In determining what to do about misconduct, a supervisor has much discretion and a variety of disciplinary actions from which to choose. The following briefly discusses the different aspects of common types of discipline.

• Counseling
This is the least serious type of discipline, and should be used for relatively minor misconduct for a first offense when a supervisor believes the employee will respond. When counseling occurs, it is entirely appropriate for the supervisor to make a written record of the fact that the counseling happened, what was said and any employee reaction.

For minor types of misconduct, alternative sanctions may serve as a deterrent to the employee not to repeat the same misconduct in the future.

Categories of Disciplinary/ Adverse Actions

- Counseling

- Letter of Warning

- Admonishment

- Reprimand

- Suspension

- Demotion

- Removal

• Letter of Warning

This is somewhat more serious than a counseling session, because it is in writing. A letter of warning is a formal means of putting an employee on notice that certain conduct is not acceptable. Sometimes, a letter of warning may be used to counsel an employee about conduct the employee already knows is unacceptable. Other times, a letter of warning may be used to put an employee on notice that certain conduct is unacceptable, especially when the employee might be unaware of the offending nature of his actions.

• Admonishment

An admonishment is more serious than a counseling session or a letter of warning, only because it in fact indicates some blameworthiness on the part of the employee. In other words, the admonishment specifically indicates that the employee has done something wrong and repeated instances of the same type of misconduct may result in more serious punishment. It is entirely appropriate for an admonishment to be confirmed in writing or to be reduced to some sort of document the supervisor may retain. An admonishment should not be maintained in an employee's Official Personnel File (OPF).

• Reprimand

A reprimand is a more serious means of discipline. It is a written statement from a supervisory authority indicating that the employee has committed some act of wrongdoing. It is official and is ordinarily placed in the employee's OPF. A reprimand may be examined by anyone, including a prospective employer from another federal agency, who has access to the employee's OPF. OPM regulations prohibit maintaining a written reprimand in an OPF for more than three years, and many agencies or collective bargaining agreements limit the length of time a reprimand may remain in an OPF to two years; see OPM Operating Manual, The Guide to Personnel Record Keeping, which replaced FPM Supp. 293-31.

• Suspension

A suspension without pay is a significant disciplinary action. For federal civil service employees, the suspension remains a permanent part of the official personnel file. Thus the suspension, when imposed, should not be taken lightly. Suspensions of more than 14 days may be appealed to the MSPB. (5 U.S.C. 7513)

• Demotion

A demotion, in most instances, is far more serious than a suspension. A demotion for misconduct does not carry with it any pay retention and the employee is paid (after the demotion) at the lower pay level of the grade to which demoted. Most often, the demotion results in a far more significant loss of income over an employee's career than does the suspension. The demotion is an appropriate penalty when the employee's action indicates that he can no longer perform at the previous grade level. (5 U.S.C. 7513)

• Removal

A removal is the most serious penalty. In fact, labor relations professionals sometimes refer to it as "economic capital punishment." It is a very serious penalty, often affecting the removed person for the remainder of his working career. It should only be imposed in those cases in which less serious forms of disciplinary action will not be effective. (5 U.S.C. 7513 and 5 C.F.R. 752.401)

Conclusion

The federal personnel system encourages the maintenance of a safe, productive and ethical workplace by authorizing supervisors to take disciplinary action against employees who engage in misconduct. Supervisors should strive to be fair in rendering their decisions regarding the imposition of penalties for misconduct. The weighing and balancing of the appropriate *Douglas* factors will help ensure fairness and uniformity of disciplinary decisions and achieve the appropriate result of correcting misconduct and discouraging misconduct in the future.

Supervisors should strive to be fair in rendering decisions regarding the imposition of penalties for misconduct.

Overcoming Common Employee Defenses To A Misconduct Case

Overcoming Common Employee Defenses To A Misconduct Case

When an agency imposes discipline on an employee in a misconduct case, it is quite common for the employee to challenge the agency's action by raising an affirmative defense, such as harmful procedural error or unlawful discrimination. The employee may succeed in such a challenge if he can prove that the agency's action was unlawful or improper. The employee has the burden of proving his affirmative defense by a preponderance of the evidence. If the employee is unable to meet this standard, the agency's action will be upheld if the agency is then able to prove that the charges alleged are supported by a preponderance of the evidence. (5 U.S.C. 7701(c)(1)(B))

The best way to overcome an employee's affirmative defense is to make sure that any action taken by the agency complies with the agency's procedures and is otherwise in accordance with federal law. In order to identify and eliminate problems, a supervisor should always consult an agency attorney or employee relations specialist prior to initiating a disciplinary action. It is important to keep in mind, however, that the employee has the burden of proof for an affirmative defense. Some examples of common affirmative defenses raised by employees follow.

Harmful Procedural Error

All procedural errors are not "harmful."

When an agency makes a procedural mistake in processing its case against the employee, the charge may be susceptible to the affirmative defense of harmful procedural error. In order to succeed on this defense, the employee must demonstrate that he was harmed by the agency's error. This means the employee must show that the result reached in the case could have been different had the error not occurred.

An obvious example of harmful procedural error would be if the agency took action against an employee based upon a charge not stated in the notice proposing the disciplinary action. The employee then would have been deprived of the opportunity to defend himself.

All procedural errors are not "harmful," however. Examples of commonly alleged harmful procedural errors are stale charges, failure to advise an employee of his right to representation, disciplining an employee for the same charge more than once (double jeopardy), deficient notice of charges, inadequate reply period, improper bias on the part of the deciding official, and failure of the deciding official to consider an employee's response to the charges. For any of these procedural errors to be a successful affirmative defense, the employee must specifically show how the error could have affected the decision to take the adverse action. For a more detailed analysis of harmful procedural error, *see Mercer v. Dep't. of Health and Human Services,* 772 F.2d 856 (Fed. Cir. 1985); *Parker v. Defense Logistics Agency,* 1 M.S.P.R. 505 (1980).

☑ CASE IN POINT
The Department of the Interior proposed to remove Ted from his position as park ranger, but Ted was not advised of his right to be represented by a lawyer. The charges against him were highly technical, and Ted felt that he would benefit from the assistance of an attorney. He thought, however, that he had to represent himself. After Ted was removed, he learned of his right to counsel and appealed his case to the Merit Systems Protection Board (MSPB). The MSPB will reverse the agency's decision on

this basis alone if Ted demonstrates that the charges against him might not have been sustained by the agency had he been advised of his right to counsel; see, e.g., Loveland v. Dep't. of the Air Force, 37 M.S.P.R. 554 (1988).

Mistake Of Law

An agency disciplinary action that is not in accordance with law may be successfully challenged by an aggravated employee. This type of action is distinguishable from harmful procedural error and instead involves an inquiry into whether the agency's decision is unlawful in its entirety or, in other words, whether the agency's action lacks legal authority. The burden of showing that an agency action is not in accordance with law rests with the employee.

☑ CASE IN POINT

The Air Force sought to terminate a probationary civil service employee on the precise date the employee would have completed his first year of work. It failed, however, to specify whether the termination was to be effective prior to the end of the employee's one-year tour of duty on that date. The MSPB held that it could not assume that the termination was intended to take effect prior to the time the employee's one-year probationary period ended. As a result, the agency had violated the notice and opportunity to respond requirements for termination of a non-probationary federal employee and so the agency's action lacked legal authority; see Stephen v. Dep't. of Air Force, 47 M.S.P.R. 672 (1991).

Prohibited Personnel Practices

An employee may also successfully challenge discipline imposed against him by proving that the agency's action is the result of a prohibited personnel practice, such as discrimination or whistleblower reprisal. The types of conduct that constitute prohibited personnel practices are defined in Title 5 of the United States Code. (5 U.S.C. 2302(b))

As a practical matter, prohibited personnel practices are limitations on supervisors and managers who have authority to take, direct others to take, recommend, or approve any federal personnel action. The head of each agency is responsible for ensuring that prohibited personnel practices are not committed.

Prohibited personnel practices may be alleged as an affirmative defense by the employee, or used as a basis for taking disciplinary action against supervisors/managers who commit them. A supervisor who commits a prohibited personnel practice may be disciplined by his agency or prosecuted by the Office of Special Counsel (OSC).

The OSC was created under the Civil Service Reform Act of 1978 to protect the merit system and federal employees. OSC has authority to investigate allegations of prohibited personnel practices, to prosecute supervisors who commit prohibited personnel practices, and to seek corrective action for employees against whom such practices have been committed. OSC prosecutorial actions against supervisors are discussed in greater detail in Chapter 19.

Briefly, it is a prohibited personnel practice to:

- Discriminate against any employee or applicant for employment on the basis of race, color, religion, sex, age, national origin, marital status, or mental or physical handicap;

- Solicit or consider any written or oral statement or recommendation concerning an employee who is under consideration for a personnel action (such as an appointment, promotion, transfer or adverse action) unless the statement is based on the first-hand knowledge of the person making the statement, or consists only of an evaluation of the work performance, ability, aptitude or general qualifications of the person, or an evaluation of the character, loyalty, or suitability of the person;

- Coerce employees to engage in political activities, including providing contributions or services to a specific group or politician, or take action against an employee or applicant for refusing to engage in political activities;

- Deceive or willfully interfere with a person's right to compete for employment (e.g., knowingly telling a person that the time for applying for a vacancy has expired when it has not, in order to prevent that person's consideration for the position);

- Influence a person to withdraw from competition for a position for the purpose of improving or injuring another person's prospects for employment;

- Grant an unauthorized preference or advantage to an employee for the purpose of improving or injuring another person's prospects for employment (e.g., creating an unnecessary position to hire a friend for the purpose of improving the friend's chances of applying for and receiving a promotion, or limiting or expanding the scope of competition in a promotion action solely to benefit a particular person);

- Make decisions concerning the appointment, employment or promotion of a relative if the prospective position is under the supervision, jurisdiction or control of the deciding official;

- Take or fail to take, or threaten to take or fail to take, a personnel action against an employee due to the employee's whistleblowing activities (See Chapter 13);

- Take or fail to take, or threaten to take or fail to take, a personnel action against an employee due to the employee's (a) filing of a lawful appeal, complaint or grievance; (b) testifying for or lawfully assisting another person's filing of a lawful appeal, complaint or grievance; (c) lawfully cooperating with or disclosing information to the Inspector General or the Special Counsel; or (d) refusing to obey an order that would require a person to violate a law;

- Discriminate against an employee on the basis of conduct that has no bearing on his job performance or on the job performance of others (e.g., off-duty lawful, sexual conduct), except that the agency may consider the employee's conviction of a crime under the laws of any state or the federal government in determining the employee's suitability or fitness for duty, and

- Take any personnel action which violates a law, rule, or regulation implementing federal merit system principles as set forth in 5 U.S.C. 2301.

Prohibited personnel practices are discussed in this chapter only in the context of their use as an affirmative defense in an appeal of an adverse action within the jurisdiction of the MSPB.

In order for an employee to raise the affirmative defense of a prohibited personnel practice at the MSPB, the employee must first establish that a "personnel action" within the meaning of 5 U.S.C. 2302(a)(2) was taken against him. For purposes of disciplinary adverse actions appealable to the MSPB, personnel actions within the Board's jurisdiction include, for example, removal, demotion or suspension of more than 14 days.

Not all adverse personnel actions at 5 U.S.C. 2302(a)(2) are appealable to the MSPB. For example, a suspension of 14 days or less is not appealable to the MSPB.

An employee may, however, challenge such non-appealable adverse actions through agency grievance procedures. In such challenges, the employee may raise the affirmative defense that the personnel action taken was a prohibited personnel practice, as long as the adverse action complained of concerned a personnel action listed at 5 U.S.C. 2302(a)(2). For example, an employee grieving a five-day suspension (a personnel action within 5 U.S.C. 2302(a)(2)) through agency grievance procedures may defend against the suspension by claiming it was taken against him in reprisal for his refusal to engage in a political activity, a personnel action prohibited by 5 U.S.C. 2302(b)(3).

There is one caveat. An employee challenging any adverse action (appealable or non-appealable to the MSPB) as reprisal for his whistleblowing, a prohibited personnel action under 5 U.S.C. 2302(b)(8), may ultimately appeal the action to the MSPB under the Whistleblower Protection Act of 1989, regardless of the nature of the action, so long as it is a personnel action listed at 5 U.S.C. 2302(a)(2). Thus, an employee may ultimately appeal a five-day suspension to the MSPB if he is defending against it by claiming it is reprisal for whistleblowing activities. A more detailed discussion of one of the most common prohibited personnel practices, retaliation against an employee for engaging in whistleblowing activities, is presented in Chapter 13.

> The most effective
> way of avoiding
> a charge of
> a prohibited
> personnel practice
> is to ensure that
> the reasons for
> agency action are
> proper and well-
> documented.

☑ CASE IN POINT

Jane thinks that her supervisor, Alex, is misrepresenting travel expenses and making false claims on his travel vouchers based upon things she has observed him doing. Jane reports her suspicions to her agency's IG office and Alex is subsequently interviewed by an investigator. After this interview, Alex calls Jane into his office and tells her he knows that it was she who reported him to the IG. He indicates his displeasure at her actions and tells her he is going to be keeping an eye on her. Thereafter, Alex scrutinizes Jane's work and begins criticizing her performance, even though he had previously told her that her work was excellent. A few months later, Alex puts Jane on notice that her performance is below Minimally Successful on a critical element. Ultimately, Jane is removed for allegedly poor performance, even though prior to her reporting her suspicions to the IG, Alex had consistently rated Jane as a distinguished performer. If Jane appeals her removal and raises whistleblower reprisal as a defense to the removal action, she will prevail if she can establish her reporting Alex to the IG was a contributing factor in the decision to discipline her; see, e.g., Special Counsel v. Hathaway, 49 M.S.P.R. 595 (1991); Special Counsel v. Eidmann, 49 M.S.P.R. 614 (1991), aff'd, 976 F.2d 1400 (Fed. Cir. 1992).

The agency may defend against an allegation that an action constitutes a prohibited personnel practice by demonstrating that the agency's actions were for legitimate management reasons. This defense is articulated in different ways: in discrimination cases, the agency may defend against an allegation of discrimination by demonstrating that the personnel action was for legitimate, non-discriminatory reasons; in whistleblower reprisal actions, the agency may defend against a showing that retaliation was a "contributing factor" to the personnel actions complained of by producing "clear and convincing evidence" that the personnel action would have been effected notwithstanding any issue of retaliation.

In view of the nature of this affirmative defense, it is obvious that the most effective way of avoiding a charge of a prohibited personnel practice is to ensure that the reasons for agency actions are proper and well-documented.

As discussed, some types of prohibited personnel practices, such as whistleblower reprisal, require a finding that the supervisor's actions with respect to personnel decisions were motivated by retaliatory intent. Accordingly, statements and actions that reflect anger towards a whistleblower may be used as evidence to support an allegation of whistleblower reprisal.

While a supervisor should not be afraid to make personnel decisions that affect whistleblowers, he should be careful not to express anger or any other strong emotion about whistleblowing activities in dealings with the whistleblower. He also should avoid discussing the individual's whistleblowing allegations.

Processing A Misconduct Case

Processing A Misconduct Case

Familiarity with the process assures that no surprises develop if an employee appeals.

Admonishments And Reprimands

Once the decision is made to proceed with disciplinary action, the supervisor should understand how the adverse action system operates and what the supervisor's responsibilities are under that system. It is of the utmost importance at this stage that coordination be made with the appropriate professional in the agency responsible for providing advice on these types of personnel matters. In some agencies the appropriate person is an employee or labor management relations specialist. In others, it may be someone in the General Counsel's office.

The most serious disciplinary actions are appealable to the Merit Systems Protection Board (MSPB). In some agencies a collective bargaining agreement exists, which gives the union the option of appealing an adverse action decision to either the MSPB or an arbitrator. In either case, the MSPB is the agency charged with interpreting federal personnel law, and Board precedent is binding on the agency or an arbitrator.

This chapter discusses the procedures for processing the various types of adverse actions both within the agency and at the MSPB. Familiarity with this process is helpful in assuring that no surprises develop as an employee appeals an adverse action. Also, awareness of the following guidelines helps to fully prepare supervisors to meet their responsibilities under the process.

For relatively minor instances of misconduct, the supervisor may choose to reprimand or admonish the employee. In such cases the supervisor must prepare the written reprimand or admonishment in accordance with the agency's procedures and, if the employee is a bargaining unit employee and is represented by a union, in accordance with any collective bargaining agreement.

The supervisor must provide the employee with an opportunity to respond in writing to the reprimand or admonishment, and state his account of the facts. The employee may file a grievance under the agency grievance procedure or the union contract, and the matter will be reviewed by higher agency officials. If the employee is in a bargaining unit with union representation, the union may opt to have an outside arbitrator review the decision to impose an admonishment or reprimand.

A reprimand is more serious than an admonishment. In most cases, a reprimand is placed in the employee's official personnel file for a period not to exceed three years; see FPM Supp. 293-31. In many agencies the period does not exceed two years. During the time the reprimand is in the official personnel file, anyone who legitimately has access to the employee's OPF may review the reprimand and make personnel decisions based upon it. Thus, a reprimand is a serious matter, which may have a significant long term effect on an employee's career.

Flow Chart of Minor Disciplinary Actions

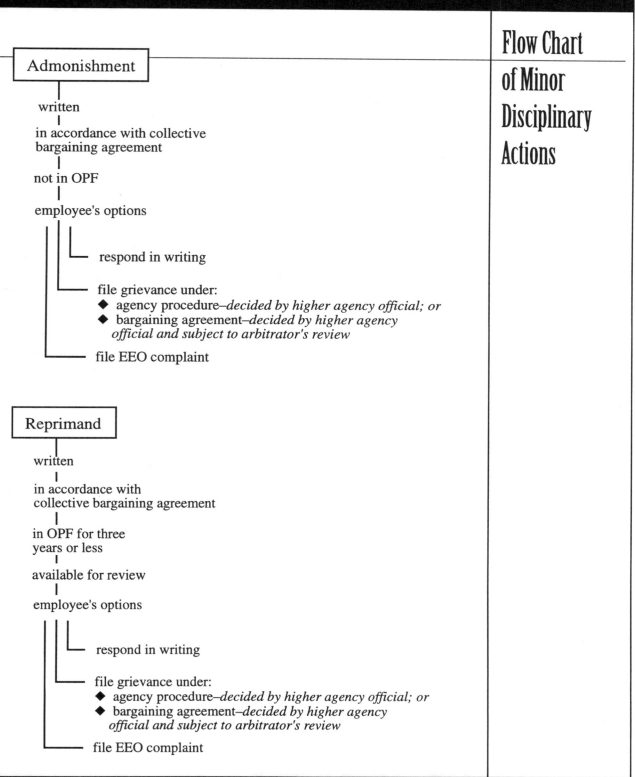

Admonishment

written

in accordance with collective bargaining agreement

not in OPF

employee's options

- respond in writing

- file grievance under:
  - ◆ agency procedure–*decided by higher agency official; or*
  - ◆ bargaining agreement–*decided by higher agency official and subject to arbitrator's review*

- file EEO complaint

Reprimand

written

in accordance with collective bargaining agreement

in OPF for three years or less

available for review

employee's options

- respond in writing

- file grievance under:
  - ◆ agency procedure–*decided by higher agency official; or*
  - ◆ bargaining agreement–*decided by higher agency official and subject to arbitrator's review*

- file EEO complaint

Suspensions Of 14 Days Or Less

The employee may not appeal a suspension of 14 days or less.

In cases where an employee is suspended for 14 days or less, the employee may not appeal to the MSPB. The agency must provide the employee with a written notice containing its reasons for suspending the employee. In addition, the employee must be provided with a reasonable time to respond in writing to the specific reasons stated and to raise any defense. At a minimum, the employee must have at least one day to respond to the proposed suspension. The agency must advise the employee of his right to be represented by an attorney or other representative of his choosing. (5 U.S.C. 7503)

If the agency does not follow correct procedures, the employee might challenge the failure to follow correct procedures in court. If the agency used the wrong procedures, the court will at most send the matter back to the agency for a new action.

The employee may not challenge in court the agency's reasons for the suspension. The employee may challenge the agency's actual reasons for suspending him only through the grievance procedure, or by filing an Equal Employment Opportunity (EEO) or Special Counsel complaint.

A suspension is a serious personnel action, even more serious than a reprimand, because a suspension results in an employee losing pay. The documents reflecting the loss of pay and the reasons for it remain a permanent part of a federal employee's official file. Thus, an employee who has been suspended will always have that fact known by management officials in assessing future personnel decisions.

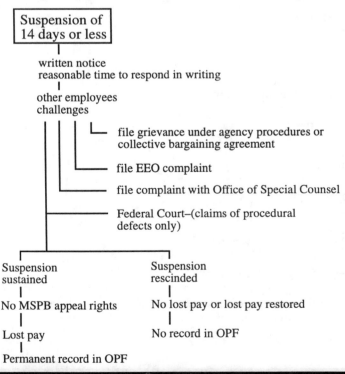

Demotions, Suspensions Of More Than 14 Days, And Removals

When the supervisor determines that the serious penalties of demotion, suspension of more than 14 days, or removal are warranted, the agency must strictly comply with the detailed statutory procedures for imposing an adverse action. When this type of penalty is imposed, the employee is entitled to written notice of the specific reasons for the agency's action. The employee is also entitled to at least 30 days advance notice of the decision taking effect. During this notice period, the employee ordinarily remains in a duty status. (See discussion that follows for those situations in which an employee can be immediately removed.) In addition, the employee has the right to respond orally and in writing to the agency's action. By statute, the employee is entitled to a minimum of seven (7) days to respond, but this response period is often extended by the agency in cases where the employee makes a reasonable request for an extension. (5 U.S.C. 7513) Most agencies initially allow an employee at least 10 to 14 days to respond.

The employee is entitled to make an oral reply before an individual who is in a position to make or recommend a final decision on the proposed adverse action. (5 C.F.R. 752.404(c)(2)) Normally, the employee makes his oral reply before the agency's deciding official or the deciding official's designee. The agency should be certain that the oral reply is recorded either verbatim by a court reporter or by careful note-taking. If the employee appeals the agency's action to the MSPB, the agency must provide the MSPB with a written summary of what occurred at the oral reply. (5 U.S.C. 7513(e)) A verbatim transcript is strongly recommended because it limits disagreement over what was said by either party at the oral reply.

In all cases where the agency proposes an adverse action against an employee, the employee has the right to be represented by an attorney or other representative of the employee's choosing. This right to counsel applies to both the oral and written reply at the agency and at the MSPB. These serious adverse actions are fully appealable to the MSPB.

> The employee has the right to be represented by an attorney or other representative.

Immediate Removal Of An Employee From The Worksite

As mentioned above, an employee against whom a serious adverse action is proposed is ordinarily entitled to 30 days advance notice, during which time the employee remains in a duty status. In some circumstances, however, a federal employee's conduct may be so serious that permitting the employee to remain in a duty status is not required.

OPM regulations specifically authorize an agency to place an employee in other than a normal duty status if the employee's presence poses a threat to the employee or others, results in loss or damage to government property, or otherwise jeopardizes a legitimate government interest. (5 C.F.R. 752.404(b)(3))

Under these circumstances, the agency has the option of assigning the employee to alternate duties where the employee is no longer a threat, allowing the employee to take leave, curtailing the notice period under the crime provision (discussed below), or placing the employee in a paid non-duty status for such time as is necessary to effect the adverse action.

Crime Provision

☑ **CASE IN POINT**
Tom, a federal employee, has lost his temper on the job and assaulted his supervisor. In the course of the assault, Tom also broke a chair, a piece of government property. The agency need not keep Tom in a duty status and may immediately remove him from the worksite and bar him from returning, pending resolution of the adverse action; cf. Gonzales v. Dep't. of Treasury, 37 M.S.P.R. 589 (1988).

The crime provision allows the agency to shorten the usual 30-day notice period to seven days when an agency reasonably believes that an employee has committed an act for which a sentence of imprisonment can be imposed. (5 C.F.R. 752.404 (b)(3)(iii)) Ordinarily, to invoke the crime provision, the agency would need more information than just the fact that an employee had been arrested or was under investigation. However, a grand jury indictment or magistrate's determination of probable cause is usually sufficient evidence for an agency to use in determining that the employee's notice period may be shortened under the crime provision. The agency may also independently develop facts to show that the employee has committed an illegal act, which carries a possible jail sentence.

The importance of the shortened notice period allowed under the crime provision is that it provides a mechanism for removal of the employee from the workplace and termination of the employee's pay within a relatively short time period.

Indefinite Suspension

Authorized by the MSPB, this adverse action allows an employee to be on suspension without pay.

An indefinite suspension is an adverse action authorized by the MSPB, which allows an employee to be placed on suspension without pay if there is reason to believe that the employee has committed an act for which a criminal sentence of imprisonment can be imposed. (5 C.F.R. 752.402(e)) The procedural safegaurds afforded in cases where the Agency has proposed a demotion, removal or time-limited suspension must also be afforded to the employee facing a proposed indefinite suspension. (5 C.F.R. 752.401(a)(2)) The employee must be specifically advised why the indefinite suspension is being imposed and notified of the event that will mark the end of the indefinite suspension.

Usually this event is the termination of criminal prosecution. However, the mere fact of pending criminal charges is insufficient to justify the agency's failure to consider an action less severe than indefinite suspension. The agency must give some consideration to the nature of the charges and determine whether a lesser action would, in fact, be ineffective; *see Brown v. Dep't. of Justice,* 715 F.2d 662 (D.C. Cir. 1983).

☑ **CASE IN POINT**
A Correctional Officer at the Metropolitan Correctional Center in New York was indefinitely suspended, based on information filed in district court that the employee violated 18 U.S.C. 1791 when he provided a veal cutlet sandwich to an inmate. A person convicted of violating this criminal code could be sentenced to prison for no more than six months. The agency's imposition of the indefinite suspension was reversed by the MSPB on the basis that there were alternative means of protecting the

agency's interest. The MSPB also found that an indefinite suspension action may not stand if a less severe action would suffice. Thus, the MSPB concluded that the indefinite suspension in this instance did not promote the efficiency of the service; see Vega v. Dep't. of Justice, 37 M.S.P.R. 115 (1988).

However, the MSPB has upheld the imposition of an indefinite suspension during the investigation of whether an employee is entitled to a security clearance, despite the absence of reasonable cause to believe that the employee was guilty of a crime; see *Jones v. Dep't. of Navy,* 48 M.S.P.R. 680 (1991).

Ex Parte Communications

If the employee demonstrates to the MSPB that in processing its case against him the agency did not give him adequate due process (fair treatment), the MSPB may reverse the agency's action. For this reason, supervisors should avoid impermissible ex parte communications with deciding officials while the employee's case is being considered by the agency.

Ex parte communications are prohibited.

The term "ex parte communications" means contacts by one participant in a case with the person deciding the matter (including judges and deciding officials) with no notice of the contact to the other participant. Such communications are prohibited in most administrative and court actions due to the risk that the party who is excluded from the communication may, by his absence, be disadvantaged by information exchanged between his opponent and the judge or other deciding official.

To prevent losing a case due to the employee's charge that his supervisor and the deciding official engaged in impermissible ex parte communications, agency personnel should avoid any such contacts if they are designed to influence the deciding official. Of course, some discussion is permitted and ordinarily occurs in most agencies. However, the interested supervisor and other proposing officials should be careful not to attempt to influence the deciding official without the presence, knowledge and participation of the employee and/or his representative.

☑ CASE IN POINT

An employee was removed from his position with the Department of the Navy based on charges that he submitted false claims to the federal government and wrongfully obtained funds from the federal government by submission of these false claims. The information which formed the basis for the charges was obtained through a 21-day surveillance of the employee by the agency.

The surveillance of the employee was initiated by the employee's supervisor just 18 days after the employee filed a grievance against the supervisor. The employee was provided the opportunity to present an oral reply to the charges to an agency official designated as the hearing officer. The supervisor did not participate in the hearing, yet several days after the hearing, the supervisor phoned the hearing officer, urging him to "hurry up" in making his report concerning the charges.

Subsequently, the hearing officer provided the supervisor with his four-page recommendation letter. The supervisor forwarded the recommendation to the deciding official. The supervisor then telephoned the deciding official's aide, on more than one occasion, urging him to see that the decision would be issued without delay. The supervisor also advised the deciding official's aide that, in his opinion, the recommendation of the hearing officer was correct and the employee should be removed from office. The supervisor then sent his recommendation urging that the employee be removed by the deciding official. The deciding official issued a decision removing the employee from office.

The removal of the employee was struck down on appeal based upon the supervisor's ex parte communications with the deciding official and the deciding official's aide. The supervisor's improper ex parte communications were deemed unfair because they denied the employee his rights under the due process clause of the U.S. Constitution; see Sullivan v. Dep't. of the Navy, 720 F.2d 1266 (Fed. Cir. 1983).

Considerations Before Taking Misconduct Adverse Action

- Assess the problem and determine whether it is performance or conduct related.

- Obtain the assistance of the personnel, employee relations or legal office, if appropriate.

- Determine whether progressive discipline is appropriate.

- Consider whether drug or alcohol abuse are contributing to the employee's misconduct. If so, provide the employee reasonable accommodation by referring him to the Employee Assistance Program (EAP). (See Chapter 17.)

- Conduct appropriate counseling for petty offenses.

- Document in writing specific instances of misconduct or counseling, including exact dates of the misconduct and counseling, as well as what the employee was told and how the employee responded. (See Chapter 3.)

- Propose an adverse action against the employee with the assistance of the employee relations and/or legal office.

- In the case of a proposed lengthy suspension, demotion or removal, make sure the employee is advised of and receives all of his procedural rights, including 30-days notice, an opportunity to respond orally and/or in writing, the right to legal representation, and the opportunity to review the evidence upon which the agency is basing its action.

- Make sure there are documents and/or testimony which support the charges.

- Consider relevant *Douglas* mitigating factors when determining appropriate penalties. (See Chapter 5.)

- If the misconduct occurred when the employee was off-duty, make sure there is a nexus between the off-duty misconduct and the employee's employment.

- Impose the least severe penalty necessary to promote the efficiency of the service. Exhaust all reasonable measures to rehabilitate the employee prior to terminating the employee.

Checklist for Misconduct Adverse Action

✔	Assess nature of problem or conduct.
✔	Obtain appropriate agency assistance.
✔	Determine appropriateness of progressive discipline.
✔	Provide reasonable accommodation for alcohol or drug problem.
✔	Conduct counseling for petty offenses.
✔	Propose adverse action with assistance of employee relations.
✔	Advise and provide employee with all procedural rights.
✔	Use documents and/or testimony to support charge.
✔	Determine least sever penalty using *Douglas* factors.
✔	Establish nexus between off-duty misconduct and employment.
✔	Document all instances of misconduct and counseling.
✔	Exhaust all reasonable measures to rehabilitate employee before termination.

Overview Of The Federal Performance Appraisal System

Overview Of The Federal Performance Appraisal System

The enactment of the Civil Service Reform Act of 1978 (CSRA) was a highlight of the Carter Administration. The law brought much-needed uniformity to the federal workplace, in part by establishing the federal performance appraisal system. The performance appraisal system is currently used by virtually every federal agency to evaluate the job performance of each employee on a regular basis. These appraisals may also be used as a basis for significant personnel actions, including promotions, assignments and adverse actions. (5 U.S.C. 4301-4305 (1978))

A primary objective of the performance appraisal system is to provide each employee with feedback from his supervisor concerning the quality of the employee's work. If a supervisor indicates on the performance appraisal that the employee's performance is exceptional, under certain circumstances the employee may qualify for monetary awards or promotion. If the employee's performance is weak in one or more areas, the performance appraisal is used to notify the employee of deficiencies that must be improved.

Managers and supervisors should not underestimate the significance of the performance appraisal system as a tool for rehabilitating or removing problem employees.

Notably, enactment of the CSRA substantially modified the burden of proof necessary to sustain a performance adverse action. In return, additional requirements were placed on managers to advise employees in advance of what was expected of them. These requirements, now imposed by statute for taking performance-based adverse actions, are nothing more than a statement of what a good manager should do to attempt to rehabilitate an employee who is not adequately performing his job.

360-Degree Performance Appraisals

One new development in the area of performance appraisals, which is currently being tested on a trial basis in a few agencies, is the 360-degree performance appraisal. The concept behind the 360-degree performance appraisal is to provide employees with feedback concerning their performance from sources other than the traditional top-down, supervisory review. For example, the rating officer might receive feedback from the employee's subordinates, team members, and customers during the appraisal process. Typically, subordinates, team members, and customers will provide this information to the employee's rating officer, who will consider it when determining the appropriate performance rating. While no agency has permanently implemented the 360-degree performance appraisal, it may be adopted by agencies in the near future. Several demonstration projects are now taking place.

One issue that remains unresolved is the extent to which rating officers should rely on the comments of subordinates, team members, and customers when determining an unacceptable performance rating for an employee. The possibility exists that rating officers will determine an employee's performance rating solely on the basis of the comments of subordinates, team members and customers.

However agencies resolve this issue, rating officers should bear in mind the "substantial evidence" standard applicable in performance-based adverse actions at the Merit Systems

Protection Board (MSPB), discussed below. Briefly stated, for an agency to sustain a performance-based adverse action at the MSPB, the agency must show by substantial evidence that performance deficiencies existed, the employee was afforded a meaningful opportunity to improve, and the employee's performance did not improve. If an agency utilizes a mechanical formula, such as automatically rating an employee's performance "Unacceptable" if the employee receives a certain number of negative comments from subordinates, team members, or customers, a serious question exists whether the MSPB would find the agency had proven a performance deficiency existed by substantial evidence. To satisfy the substantial evidence standard, and to avoid this potential pitfall, agencies should specifically require rating officers to make <u>independent</u> judgments about employees' performance, rather than simply relying on a mechanical formula.

In conclusion, while 360-degree performance appraisals may prove to be a useful tool in judging and improving employees' performance, agencies should be careful not to rely solely on the comments of subordinates, team members and customers in determining appropriate performance ratings, or they run the risk of having their performance-based adverse actions overturned at the MSPB.

Substantial Evidence Rule

For an agency to support an adverse action because of misconduct, the agency must prove that each disputed fact is more likely true than not true, the "preponderance of the evidence standard." (See Chapters 3 and 7.) In performance cases, the agency still has the burden of proof at the MSPB, but by a reduced "substantial evidence" standard. Substantial evidence means that degree of evidence which a reasonable person could accept when considering the record as a whole. (5 C.F.R. 1201.56(c)(1)) This means, in practice, that even if the employee presents a good argument that he performed his job, the supervisor's judgment that the employee did not accomplish his job will be accepted unless the supervisor's opinion is unreasonable or has no factual support.

This evidentiary standard has resulted in nearly all performance-based adverse actions being sustained by the MSPB, at least on the issue of whether the employee adequately performed his job duties. In ruling on performance cases, the MSPB routinely refuses to substitute its judgment for that of the supervisor on the significant issue of whether an employee's performance was acceptable. Despite this, a 1990 General Accounting Office (GAO) study shows that few performance-based adverse actions are taken. (See Performance Management: How Well is the Government Dealing with Poor Performance (GAO/GGD 91-7, October 1990)). The often heard complaint that the system does not allow effective action against non-performers has been proven untrue by MSPB decisions.

Procedural Requirements

If used correctly, the performance appraisal system will encourage an employee who is not performing his job adequately to correct his performance deficiencies.

For those employees who fail to perform, the performance appraisal system gives a federal manager an effective method to remove the employee. The only real way for a supervisor/manager to fail with a performance-based adverse action is to act with improper motives or to fail to comply with procedural requirements.

In the landmark decision, *Eibel v. Dep't. of the Navy,* 857 F.2d 1439 (Fed. Cir. 1988), the Court of Appeals for the Federal Circuit recognized the importance of procedural protections. In that case, the court stated that a federal employee has no other protections than the procedures in a performance case, and the court found that agencies must comply with procedural protections, particularly the development of adequate and proper performance standards.

This makes sense. A good performance standard is nothing more than notice to the employee of what is expected of him and an indication of how management views the employee's work in conjunction with the agency's mission. Without adequate notice to the employee, the agency should not be permitted to take an adverse action for performance, especially since such actions have a low requirement for proof. With adequate notice, however, a manager or supervisor has almost unlimited discretion. Chapter 9 discusses in greater detail the legal requirements in developing valid performance standards.

Other procedural requirements include the communication of performance standards to the employee, the granting of an adequate opportunity period (PIP) to improve unacceptable performance (see Chapter 10), and the effective appraisal of an employee who is failing to perform. Also, the Office of Personnel Management (OPM) must approve the agency performance appraisal system under which the performance standards are developed and adverse actions are taken. (5 C.F.R. 430.210 (1996)) All affected agencies now have OPM approved plans (see next page).

The Performance Appraisal System Coverage

With the exception of U.S. Postal Service workers (see Chapter 18), most federal workers are covered by the performance appraisal system. Each agency develops and implements its own performance appraisal system, which has been approved by OPM. In addition, there are slight variations on the systems used for different categories of federal employees. For example, the regulations which define the system used for evaluating General Schedule (GS-15 and below) and Prevailing Rate (wage board) employees are set forth in 5 C.F.R. 430.201-430.210 (1996). The regulations for Senior Executive Service (SES) employees are contained in 5 C.F.R. 430.301-430.310 (1996).

Performance Regulations for Different Employee Categories

General Schedule and Prevailing Rate, 5 C.F.R. 430.201-430.210 (1996).

SES   5 C.F.R. 430.301-430.310 (1996).

> Used correctly, the performance appraisal system will encourage an employee who is not performing his job adequately to correct his performance deficiencies.

Elements Of The Appraisal System

A performance standard is how a supervisor measures whether the employee met, exceeded or failed to meet his job elements.

• Critical Elements and Noncritical Elements

The OPM rules require that an agency's performance appraisal system provide each employee with a written description of his job. (5 C.F.R. 430.204(b)(1)(ii) (1996)) The duties of each position must then be divided into critical elements and noncritical elements. Critical elements include those aspects of each position that are so essential to the job that unacceptable performance of that particular aspect would make it impossible for the employee to perform his job effectively. (5 C.F.R. 430.203 (1996))

For example, an attorney working for the Department of Justice must file certain documents with the court by deadlines set by the court. If he fails to do so, the court may refuse to consider the documents as part of the government's case. Thus, filing documents in a timely fashion would be a critical element of that attorney's job description. If the attorney does not file papers in a timely fashion, the government may lose all of the cases that attorney is handling, and thus the attorney would not be effectively performing his job. In contrast, a noncritical element of a job is one that is not absolutely essential to the successful completion of the employee's job, but is sufficiently important to warrant evaluation on the employee's appraisal.

For example, an attorney may be expected to take an eight-hour course each year to study recent developments in his particular area of practice. The completion of such studies may not be essential to the attorney's ability to perform his job, yet his attendance at such courses may play a significant role in ensuring that he is using the most up-to-date law and procedures in each case he handles. Thus, the attorney's attendance or absence from such programs would have an impact on his overall effectiveness and worth to the Department of Justice.

• Performance Standards

Each critical or non-critical element must be accompanied by a performance standard. A performance standard is the measurement by which a supervisor or manager determines whether the employee met, exceeded or failed to meet his job elements. The importance of a performance standard cannot be overstated. It is the application of a performance standard to the critical element which results in the determination of whether the employee failed to meet a critical element. This important finding must be made in order to sustain a performance-based adverse action.

The most common reason an agency has difficulty sustaining a performance-based adverse action is an inadequately developed performance standard. Chapter 9 discusses performance standards in detail and provides insight into how a supervisor or manager might turn, what could otherwise be an objectionable standard, into one that has meaning and validity, both for the employee being rehabilitated and for any reviewing official.

Each appraisal system must contain at least two, but not more than five summary ratings.

• Structure of the Appraisal System

Each appraisal system provides a minimum of two (2) rating levels for each critical element. The two ratings are "unacceptable" or "not met," and "fully successful" or "met." (5 C.F.R. 430.206 (b)(7)(i) (1996) Agencies may instead have a three or a five-level rating system for each critical element. Typically a five-level rating system includes the two rating levels described above and additional rating levels to describe "minimally successful" or "marginal" performance, another level between "acceptable" and "outstanding" performance, or "highly successful" performance, and a rating to describe the highest performance level, typically called the "outstanding" performance level.

Agencies using a five-level rating system for each critical element should take care to describe "minimally successful" or "marginal" performance standards in positive terms, because a level "2" performance rating is considered "acceptable" performance for General Schedule employees and no adverse action may be initiated based on acceptable performance. Thus, negatively written standards for "marginal" but "acceptable" performance can be confusing to the employee and will likely be rejected by the MSPB or the courts if used as justification for discipline or discharge. (See Chapter 9 for a more detailed discussion and specific examples of negative or backwards standards.)

Each appraisal system must contain at least two (2), but not more than five (5), summary ratings. The required summary ratings must include an "unacceptable" level and a "fully successful" level. Agencies may identify terms as equivalent to "fully successful" in their performance management plans. (5 C.F.R. 430.206(b)(7) (1996))

If the employee receives a rating that is unacceptable in any critical element, the agency must provide the employee with a performance improvement plan or opportunity period (PIP). (5 C.F.R. 432.104 (1996))

The written PIP enumerates the employee's performance deficiencies and advises the employee of how to achieve an acceptable level of performance. The PIP is discussed in detail in Chapter 10. If the employee's performance remains unacceptable at the termination of the opportunity period, the agency may initiate an adverse action against the employee. (5 C.F.R. 432.105(a)(l) (1996)) Performance adverse actions include reassignment, reduction-in-grade, or removal of the employee, provided certain procedural safeguards are met. The procedures which must be followed before an adverse action is implemented are discussed in Chapter 11.

The following chapters more fully describe each aspect of the federal performance appraisal system and how to use that system to rehabilitate or remove the problem employee.

Developing Valid Performance Standards

Developing Valid Performance Standards

An employee's performance standards should be written clearly, simply and in unambigous terms.

DRAFTING PERFORMANCE STANDARDS

To the extent practicable, an employee's performance standards should be drafted with the joint participation of the employee and supervisor/manager. Many agencies recommend that as an initial step the employee and his supervisor discuss and develop a performance plan together. In many instances the employee provides the supervisor with a draft performance plan, and the supervisor makes modifications deemed appropriate. In other cases, the supervisor may draft a performance plan and elicit responses from the employee. In cases where two or more employees occupy similar positions, a performance plan may be drafted by the group of employees and submitted to their supervisor for his modifications and final approval. In all cases, final authority and responsibility for establishing the plan rests with the supervising or management official.

Some agencies use generic standards for all employees. Other agencies develop uniform standards for particular categories of jobs. Nonetheless, a supervisor should still discuss the performance standards with the employees. These standards may be given "content" through these discussions or memos. Also, this supplementation may be used later by a supervisor as a further explanation of what the performance standard actually means and to show that the employee knew what was expected of him.

Finally, even though an agency may have a uniform standard, nothing prevents a supervisor from advising higher-level management of improvements that could be made to the performance standard.

The Court of Appeals for the Federal Circuit warned in the landmark case of *Eibel v. Dep't. of the Navy,* 857 F.2d 1439 (Fed. Cir. 1988), that it expects agencies to learn from their experiences with the performance appraisal system and encouraged managers constantly to develop better, clearer and more objective performance standards.

PERFORMANCE STANDARDS MUST BE CLEAR AND UNAMBIGUOUS

The level of performance expected of the employee for each critical element must be clearly communicated to the employee. This means that each performance standard should be written in clear, simple, unambiguous terms. In addition, the level of performance expected of each employee must be stated in as reasonably objective, as opposed to subjective, terms as is feasible for the job.

☑ CASE IN POINT

A GS-7 Personnel Security Assistant was removed from his position for unsatisfactory performance under a critical element. The critical element required him "to conduct security suitability investigations requiring access to the facility." The standard set time limits for completion of the investigation was to be consistent with the return of information responding to inquiries made to law enforcement agencies. In other words, the standard expected was expeditious processing once the employee received the information needed to complete the investigation. On appeal to the Merit Systems Protection Board (MSPB), the employee alleged that the standard was subjective, since it did not provide exact time limits on the investigations.

The Board disagreed, finding the standard to be as objective as possible, given the above-referenced qualifying language, which essentially set due dates relative to each investigation; see Powell v. Dep't. of the Treasury, 37 M.S.P.R. 78, 81 (1988), aff'd, 864 F.2d 149 (Fed. Cir. 1988).

MANAGERS'/SUPERVISORS' PERFORMANCE STANDARDS

Drafting performance standards for jobs held by managers and supervisors requires recognizing that individual job responsibilities vary greatly, but all managers and supervisors share the common requirement of implementing their managerial duties effectively. The Office of Personnel Management (OPM) recommends that performance standards for management positions ensure that management activities are evaluated regularly and correctly. In addition, management performance standards should emphasize appropriate agency objectives and purposes. For example, priorities among managers at the Office of Management and Budget (OMB) might include cost reduction, whereas managers at the Equal Employment Opportunity Commission (EEOC) might highlight affirmative action as a priority. Finally, OPM suggests that management performance standards should clearly define the duties which are expected of each agency's managers and supervisors.

DRAFTING PERFORMANCE STANDARDS WHEN THE JOB DUTIES CANNOT BE DESCRIBED ACCURATELY OR PREDICTED IN ADVANCE

Some jobs, particularly higher-level management and supervisory jobs, cannot be subjected to precise or technical performance standards. These jobs, by definition, require some subjectivity in supervisory judgment in evaluating performance. In such circumstances the performance standards should still be drafted to be as specific as possible.

Recognizing that complete specificity cannot be obtained, the manager or supervisor of an employee with an imprecise performance standard should provide oral and/or written feedback to the employee about performance requirements and deficiencies. This feedback should be provided as frequently as necessary to inform the employee of what the supervisor expects.

In these circumstances, the MSPB and courts will consider whether the performance standard was supplemented by specific instructions. If it was, it is far more likely that the performance standard will be upheld.

Performance standards for management positions should ensure that their activities are evaluated regularly and correctly.

☑ CASE IN POINT

The MSPB considered the following performance standard for an employee who occupied a management analyst position:

Written material is prepared in accordance with established stated objectives and is clearly written, succinct and consistent with regulations and established policies. Little, if any, re-write is required and necessary approval/concurrence of finished product is easily obtained.

The MSPB found this standard to be subjective and therefore valid only if the agency provided evidence that supervisory feedback during the rating period gave the standard "content." In the absence of evidence of such feedback, the MSPB declared this particular performance standard to be too vague to be valid. Thus, the same performance standard could be found to be either valid or invalid, depending on the supervisor's oral and/or written feedback to the problem employee during the period the work was performed or during the appraisal period; see O'Neal v. Dep't. of the Army, 47 M.S.P.R. 433 (1991).

EMPLOYEE FEEDBACK

> Feedback to the employee should communicate specific standards that establish a firm benchmark for performance.

The employee should be provided feedback through: 1) specific work requirements conveyed by written instructions; 2) information concerning deficiencies and methods of improving performance; 3) memoranda describing unacceptable performance; and 4) responses to the employee's questions concerning performance.

The MSPB requires that feedback provided to the employee communicate the performance standards with sufficient specificity so as to provide the employee with a firm benchmark toward which to aim performance. The standard cannot represent an elusive goal which the agency at its pleasure may find the employee met or failed to meet.

Finally, the supervisor who develops performance standards for employees in higher-level, technical or professional jobs or who is required to use uniform agency standards, should be careful to supplement those standards with more specific instructions to the maximum extent possible. The supervisor should document the supplementation that has occurred. This will enhance the agency's chances of having a performance standard upheld if a performance-based action is necessary. The surest way to lose a performance-based adverse action is to provide the employee with a vague, subjective standard and then to have no feedback or discussion with the employee about that standard before taking an adverse action.

THE CRITICAL ELEMENT DESCRIBED IN EACH PERFORMANCE STANDARD MUST BE REASONABLE

It is essential that each critical element be described in terms that can be realistically attained by a competent employee. If the critical element is described in unreasonable terms that are impossible to achieve, the element will be deemed to be invalid. Thus, a critical element which requires an employee to type 95 words per minute with no errors would be invalid because it is impossible for most workers to achieve this level of perfection. Stated differently, performance standards that require absolute performance are invalid and cannot be used to support an adverse action; *see Bronfman v. General Services Administration,* 40 M.S.P.R. 184, 188 (1989).

In contrast, a critical element which requires an employee to type reports at 65 words per minute with no more than five errors per page would be valid, as this is a reasonable and attainable goal.

ACCEPTABLE PERFORMANCE MUST BE DESCRIBED IN POSITIVE TERMS

The MSPB and the courts have consistently held that they will not support removal of an employee if the performance standards used to judge the employee were invalid. One case in particular, *Eibel v. Dep't. of the Navy,* 857 F.2d 1439 (Fed. Cir. 1988), illustrates the type of language that agencies should avoid in drafting performance standards.

In *Eibel,* the Court of Appeals for the Federal Circuit ruled that the Navy's "marginal" performance standard did not meet the statutory requirement that it must permit accurate evaluation of the employee's job performance on the basis of objective criteria. As such, the Navy could not base its decision to remove the employee for unacceptable performance on the faulty performance standards.

The court's decision noted that the standards used were "marginal" and "highly satisfactory," rather than the proper statutory terminology of "acceptable" and "unacceptable" performance. In addition, the standards were written in a "backwards" fashion so that they described unacceptable rather than acceptable performance. In this form, the standards were subject to various interpretations and subjective evaluation.

For example, one of the critical elements of Eibel's job description required him to coordinate and develop an agenda for his agency's annual Energy Awareness Week activities. He was also required to write at least 12 articles for publication in his agency's newspaper without assistance.

The critical element which described these duties read as follows:

Highly Satisfactory Standard: Coordinate and develop agenda for annual Energy Awareness Week.

Initiate and write 12 or more energy conservation articles for Marine Corps Development and Education Command base newspaper, without assistance, to be approved by the supervisor.

Marginal Standard: No agenda for annual Energy Awareness Week is developed. No more than six energy conservation articles for the Marine Corps Development and Education Command base newspaper. Major assistance is required at least 50 percent of the time to complete articles.

> Each critical element must be described in terms that can be attained by a competent employee.
>
> Otherwise, the element will be deemed invalid.

> It is imperative
> that each agency
> periodically
> review its
> performance
> standards.

The *Eibel* standards were declared invalid because they set no minimum level for achievement of acceptable performance. Rather, Eibel's performance was rated unsatisfactory on the basis of his supervisor's subjective determination of what the standards meant.

The court pointed out that due to the manner in which the "marginal" standard was drafted, it was unclear whether an agenda had to be drafted or whether articles had to be published to achieve a satisfactory rating under this critical element. A literal reading of the standard suggested that even if Eibel did not develop the Energy Awareness Week agenda or prepare six articles for publication, he would still meet the "marginal" standard, rather than be unsatisfactory.

The law provides that performance standards must set forth objective criteria for the critical elements of a position so that the employee will know what he must do to earn a rating of "acceptable performance." In addition, the standards must not be subject to unreasonably subjective evaluation.

For example, the court pointed out that Eibel had prepared numerous articles for publication during the performance period. Since his supervisor had determined that the articles were not suitable for publication, he determined that Eibel had not satisfied the criterion. The court said that the newspaper staff, however, may have found the content of the articles newsworthy and rewritten them, if Eibel's supervisor had submitted the articles for their review. The supervisor, however, did not permit Eibel to submit the articles to the newspaper.

SUMMARY

Performance standards must provide the employee with an accurate and reasonably objective measure of the employee's level of achievement, and reasonably inform the employee of what constitutes acceptable performance. As such, it is imperative that each agency periodically review its performance standards to ensure that they comply with these requirements.

Managers and supervisors should be particularly cautious when initiating an adverse action against an employee for unacceptable performance. Before initiating such an action, managers and supervisors should ensure: 1) that the employee's performance standards were clearly communicated to the employee, and 2) that the performance action is based on valid performance standards.

An employee who challenges a removal action based on alleged poor performance generally prevails in cases where he can show that the performance standards by which his performance was measured are somehow invalid. Once an employee places the validity of the performance standards at issue, the agency must demonstrate by substantial evidence that the standards are lawful and that they were clearly communicated to the employee.

Rehabilitation Periods

Rehabilitation Periods

PIPs are a period when employees who are performing unacceptably are given an opportunity to demonstrate acceptable performance.

Once valid performance standards have been developed and communicated to the employee, the supervisor has an obligation to provide periodic feedback to the employee. This has the effect of reinforcing the performance standard to the employee and also providing content to what otherwise might be a vague and subjective performance standard.

At some point, a supervisor may determine that a particular employee is not meeting a performance standard. By definition, this employee is now a problem employee and must become the subject of supervisory attention.

A supervisor may make a determination that an employee is performing unacceptably in one or more of the critical elements at any time during the rating period. (5 C.F.R. 432.104 (1996)) as long as the employee has been performing under a particular performance standard for at least the minimum period (if any) required under the agency's procedure.

The performance appraisal statute at 5 U.S.C. 4302(b)(6) requires that an employee who is performing unacceptably be given an opportunity to demonstrate acceptable performance before an agency may effect an adverse action because of that performance. The Merit Systems Protection Board (MSPB) has ruled that proof of completion of this requirement is a part of the agency's burden at an MSPB hearing; *see Sandland v. General Services Administration,* 23 M.S.P.R. 583 (1984).

The Office of Personnel Management (OPM) has promulgated regulations telling agencies what must be done during this opportunity period. (5 C.F.R. Part 432 (1996)) For General Schedule employees this period is referred to as an "opportunity to demonstrate acceptable performance," and is commonly called a "performance improvement plan" (PIP). (5 C.F.R. 432.103(d) (1996))

Minimum Requirements Of The PIP

The PIP notice should be in writing.

The PIP has specific minimum requirements spelled out in OPM regulations, which have been further developed by the MSPB through its decisions.

The PIP period must be sufficiently long to permit an employee to demonstrate acceptable performance. Also, the agency must, at the beginning of the PIP, inform the employee of the critical element(s) in which his performance is unacceptable, and of the performance standard which must be reached in order to avoid a performance-based adverse action. In addition, as part of the employee's opportunity to demonstrate acceptable performance, the agency must offer assistance to the employee in improving unacceptable performance. (5 C.F.R. 432.104 (1996))

The PIP notice should be in writing. Thus, specific notice of the critical element, the performance standard, and what must be done to achieve acceptable performance should be provided in writing at the beginning of the opportunity period to avoid any ambiguities or questions later about what was expected of the employee.

Length Of The PIP

Care should be taken to avoid a PIP which is too short.

The regulations contain no specific requirement as to a minimum length for an opportunity period or PIP. The period must be of sufficient length to afford the employee a reasonable opportunity to demonstrate acceptable performance. (5 C.F.R. 432.104-432.105 (1996)) Many agency performance appraisal systems provide for a minimum opportunity or PIP period, and the MSPB has upheld a performance improvement plan which was as short as 30 days in length; *see Wood v. Dep't. of Navy,* 27 M.S.P.R. 659 (1985).

For higher-graded positions, where performance evaluations are more subjective, the PIP should be longer than for lower-graded positions where performance may be evaluated over a shorter period. Care should be taken to avoid a PIP which is too short. For example, if an agency requires that an employee ordinarily complete tasks within 90 days, a PIP of 30 days is obviously insufficient.

Assistance During The PIP

OPM regulations require that an agency performance appraisal system contain provisions for assisting an employee in improving performance whenever the performance is unacceptable. (5 C.F.R. 432.104 (1996)) Thus, any employee who is performing at the "unacceptable" level in one or more of the critical elements should be receiving some kind of assistance pursuant to the agency's performance appraisal plan. This assistance can include training, additional supervisory guidance, meetings with the supervisor, or other assistance to an employee. The best way to go through the PIP is for the supervisor to approach the PIP with the attitude and expectation that, in fact, the supervisor will be successful in rehabilitating the employee. If the employee detects this genuine interest and positive attitude on the part of the supervisor, the employee will be much more positive and cooperative.

In addition, a positive attitude on the part of the supervisor, and reference to specific instances where this positive attitude has been displayed, will greatly enhance the likelihood of success at the MSPB if the employee fails to improve his performance.

☑ CASE IN POINT

Sally, a Department of Transportation Federal Highway Administration employee, is a management analyst. Sally's supervisor has noticed that Sally has difficulty recognizing important issues when she prepares her reports.

Sally seems to get side-tracked on trivial or side issues and ignores the main points. Informal counseling does not work, and Sally's supervisor puts her on a PIP. The PIP letter points out specific instances where Sally has failed to recognize the important issues in prior reports. The PIP states that, at a minimum, Sally must prepare reports over the next 90-day PIP period which recognize and develop the appropriate issues. The letter provides an open-door to Sally's supervisor to discuss concerns at any time. In addition, the supervisor promises to meet every two weeks with Sally to provide specific feedback and to talk to Sally about the issues she thinks are important in each project for which she is responsible.

During the performance improvement period, the supervisor does meet with Sally every two weeks and provides her an opportunity to ask questions, helps her develop her cases, and provides feedback to her about her performance.

Despite this notice, discussion, and follow-up by the supervisor, Sally prepares four reports during the performance improvement period, three of which fail to identify and develop significant issues. All significant issues were discussed with Sally during her bi-weekly sessions with the supervisor. At this stage, Sally has had an adequate performance improvement plan and she has been provided with an opportunity to improve. An adverse action against Sally may be proposed and the supervisor's subjective opinion that Sally has failed to identify significant issues will likely be accepted by the MSPB as the basis for sustaining the adverse action; cf. Johnson v. Dep't. of Army, 44 M.S.P.R. 464 (1990).

> There is no requirement that the supervisor provide specific assistance to the employee during the PIP.

There is no requirement that the supervisor, during the opportunity period or PIP, provide specific assistance to the employee. Rather, the agency must be prepared to assist in a general way according to OPM regulations discussed above. If the PIP letter indicates that specific assistance will be provided, however, the failure of an agency to carry out its promise could be a critical deficiency, resulting in a finding that the agency failed to afford a meaningful opportunity to the employee.

In *Adorador v. Dep't. of the Air Force,* 38 M.S.P.R. 461 (1988), the MSPB cancelled the employee's removal after hearing evidence that the supervisor failed to provide the assistance she had promised in the PIP notice letter.

☑ CASE IN POINT
In the above example, Sally was provided bi-weekly meetings with her supervisor during a 90-day period. Assume that Sally has the same promise, but the supervisor only meets with her for the first meeting, which turns out to be stormy and difficult for both Sally and the supervisor. Thus, the supervisor avoids further meetings and looks for any excuse to cancel them. Under this circumstance, the MSPB is likely to find that promised assistance to Sally was not provided and that she, therefore, had an inadequate improvement period; cf. Adorador v. Dep't. of Air Force, 38 M.S.P.R. 461 (1988).

Changing The PIP Or The Performance Standards

Before an employee is placed on a PIP, the agency must make the determination that the employee's performance is unacceptable. The only way to do this is by applying the performance standards to the critical element and making an affirmative determination that the employee is not meeting that element. Because the agency must then provide the employee an opportunity to improve performance, the agency may not change the performance standard by placing more onerous requirements on the employee during the PIP than were originally required by the performance standard.

However, the agency is not precluded from explaining what was in the basic performance standard. As long as the performance standard is not changed, the agency may provide amplification or additional details about what it expects of the employee.

By doing this, the agency gives content to the performance standard and enhances the likelihood of success on an appeal.

Once the PIP period is established, the agency should allow the employee that period of time to improve. In one case, however, the MSPB did allow some changes after the implementation of the PIP.

☑ CASE IN POINT

The employee, a scientist, was placed on a six-month performance improvement plan. After about four and one-half months, the agency believed it had adequate documentation to show the employee's performance was unacceptable, so the agency shortened the PIP.   The MSPB said in this particular case that such an action was permissible because the agency had given the employee adequate time and assistance to demonstrate acceptable performance; see Luscri v. Dep't. of Army, 39 M.S.P.R. 482 (1989), aff'd, 887 F.2d 1094 (1989).

However, an agency which unreasonably shortens a PIP is doing so at its own risk.

During the PIP it is important that the agency not establish road blocks to an employee's acceptable performance. If an employee must attend meetings in order to obtain valuable information or interact with other employees to successfully complete reports on which the employee is working, the agency must continue to invite the employee to those meetings. In some cases, the MSPB has found that an employee was placed "out of a loop" by deliberate management action and, thus, was unable to perform effectively; *see Sandland v. General Services Administration,* 23 M.S.P.R. 583 (1984).

During the PIP, the employee should continue to be allowed to function normally with: 1) the same management expectations and responsibilities, and 2) the assistance that would be provided to other employees or that was provided to the problem employee before the PIP occurred. It is permissible, and is even a good idea, to provide additional assistance to the employee, but this assistance should not confuse or hinder the employee or result in making it more difficult for him to accomplish the job.

☑ CASE IN POINT

Sally's supervisor places an additional requirement on Sally that she prepare detailed reports of her activities during the PIP. This requirement did not exist before the PIP. In some instances these reports take a substantial amount of time to prepare and distract Sally from her ability to accomplish other work assignments. The supervisor has improperly hindered Sally's ability to successfully complete the PIP; cf. Boggess v. Dep't. of Air Force, 31 M.S.P.R. 461 (1986).

> Once the PIP period is established, the agency should allow the employee that period of time to improve.

Prohibited Management Actions During A PIP

The Roller Coaster

(Or what to do when an employee completes the PIP successfully and then becomes a problem employee again)

The MSPB recognizes that some employees will perform well during a PIP, realizing the urgency of the situation and knowing that if they do not perform well they might lose their jobs. Some of these employees will then lapse back into their old habits after the PIP is completed and management informs them of successful performance during the PIP.

The MSPB has held that an employee need only be placed on one PIP within a calendar year. Thus, if an employee on a 90-day PIP performs well and then two months later performs unacceptably, that employee may be subjected to an adverse action without being placed on a new PIP; *see Conti v. Dep't. of Army,* 34 M.S.P.R. 272 (1987). Note that the new instance of unacceptable performance which occurs after the successful completion of a PIP must occur within one year of the time the employee was placed on the PIP.

☑ CASE IN POINT

Earlier examples discuss Sally at the Department of Transportation who, as a management analyst, had difficulty recognizing issues in reports she provided. Assume Sally did improve during the performance improvement plan and produced four reports during the opportunity period which recognized all significant issues and, with the assistance of the supervisor during the bi-weekly meetings, resulted in Sally's improvement to an acceptable level. After the performance improvement plan was over, the supervisor kept the open-door policy, congratulated Sally on achieving an acceptable level of performance, but discontinued the bi-weekly meetings. Sally's performance immediately fell off. Over the next six weeks she submitted three reports which were similar to her initial reports. She again failed to recognize important issues and dealt with trivial or side issues. As a result, her work became unacceptable again.

Under this circumstance, Sally's supervisor may propose an immediate adverse action against her, since her deficient performance resumed within one year of the beginning of the performance improvement plan or opportunity period; cf. Addison v. Dep't. of Health and Human Services, 46 M.S.P.R. 261 (1990), aff'd, 945 F.2d 1184 (1991).

Importance Of The PIP

The Civil Service Reform Act (CSRA) specifically requires that any employee subjected to a performance-based adverse action must be given the opportunity to improve performance. The MSPB has held that this is a substantive requirement that the agency must prove it carried out by substantial evidence; *see Sandland v. General Services Administration, supra.* What this means is that as part of the agency's case, it must establish affirmatively that the employee had an adequate performance improvement plan. Failure to provide the employee with such a plan can result in reversal of the adverse action.

By following the above steps and by really trying to rehabilitate an employee who is not performing successfully, most managers and supervisors will be able to easily establish that a problem employee has been provided with an adequate PIP or opportunity to improve unacceptable performance.

Processing An Unacceptable Performance Adverse Action

FPMII
COMMUNICATIONS

Processing An Unacceptable Performance Adverse Action

A primary responsibility of any manager is to ensure that the employees working under his supervision are accomplishing their responsibilities in a timely, efficient, and effective manner. To effectuate this responsibility, the supervisor must draft performance standards that delegate specific responsibilities within his work unit to specific employees. When each employee is fulfilling his duties effectively, the work of the entire division is performed effectively. Thus, it is essential that each employee understand that if his work is not performed, or if it is not completed in an effective manner, the work of the entire agency is adversely affected.

Counseling

Counseling provides specific guidance to the employee so that later the employee cannot assert that he did not know what was expected of him.

When a manager or supervisor detects deficiencies in the performance of a subordinate employee, his primary objective should be to identify the nature of the inadequate performance. His second objective should be to make a good faith effort to assist the employee in identifying and correcting targeted deficiencies. This process should be ongoing before and during a PIP.

The federal performance appraisal system is designed to assist managers and workers in identifying specific areas for improvement. If the system is used properly, it can greatly assist an agency in increasing the productivity of its workers. For employees who remain unproductive, the system is designed to aid an agency in removing the employee.

If a supervisor recognizes a problem with an employee's performance in one or more critical elements of his job, the supervisor should immediately bring the matter to the employee's attention.

The supervisor can initially accomplish this in an informal manner; that is, the supervisor may orally bring particular problem areas to the employee's attention and provide the employee specific suggestions for how the employee should improve his performance.

Although counseling may be conducted informally, *the supervisor should always keep a written record of any such counseling sessions.* A supervisor establishes a written record by taking specific notations of how the employee's work was deficient, what the supervisor said to the employee and what, if any, responses the employee made to the supervisor's suggestions for improvement. A union contract or other informal agency procedure may require that the supervisor provide a copy of the memo to the employee.

The importance of counseling cannot be overstated. As discussed in Chapter 9, informal counseling, whether oral or in writing, can provide content to an otherwise vague and subjective performance standard. Most important, it provides specific guidance to the employee so that later the employee cannot assert that he did not know what was expected of him.

A supervisor should expect that some employees will resist counseling. The employee may believe that the supervisor is "out to get" the employee. When this happens, the supervisor should press ahead. Counseling is essential to both the employee and the agency because the employee is specifically informed of exactly what is expected, and the agency fulfills its obligation to attempt to correct deficient performance. Avoidance of these important steps could result in significant problems for the agency in an appeal to the Merit Systems Protection Board (MSPB), and ultimately may lead to a reversal of the personnel action.

Proposing Removal Or Reduction In Grade

Continued unacceptable performance after counseling may require a supervisor to implement a performance improvement plan (PIP). (See discussion in Chapter 10.) If the employee's performance does not improve during the PIP, the agency may propose a reduction in grade or removal action against the employee. (5 C.F.R. 432.105(a)(1) (1996)) The law also provides managerial discretion to reassign an employee who is performing unacceptably. It is essential that the agency strictly comply with regulatory procedures when initiating an adverse action for demotion or removal. The agency's failure to comply with each step of the procedure is a common reason agencies fail to win performance cases at the MSPB.

For example, pursuant to 5 C.F.R. 432.105(a)(4)(i)(A), the written notice proposing the adverse action must reference both specific examples of unacceptable performance and the critical element(s) of the employee's position involved in each instance of unacceptable performance. Failure to provide specific examples of unacceptable performance would constitute a defect sufficient to result in a reversal of the adverse action by the MSPB.

Time Limit For Proposing Adverse Action

An employee subjected to a performance-based adverse action is first entitled to notice of the action proposed. (5 C.F.R. 432.105(a)(4)(i)(A)) A letter dated August 2nd should say: "The agency proposes to remove you no earlier than 30 days (September 1st) from the date of this letter." This initial 30-day period is called a "notice period." The law requires that the final decision in a performance-based adverse action be made within 30 days after the advanced notice period, or its extension, has ended.

While an agency is required to provide an employee with 30 days of advance notice of the proposed action, there are some cases in which an employee may need additional time. An agency may extend the advanced notice period for up to 30 more days under regulations prescribed by the head of the agency. In the event the notice period is still inadequate, the agency may extend the notice period further, without approval from the Office of Personnel Management (OPM), if the extension is given for one of the following reasons: 1) to obtain and/or evaluate medical information when the employee has raised a medical issue in the answer to a proposed reduction in grade or removal; 2) to make arrangements for the employee's travel to the oral reply, or for the agency official's travel to hear the employee's oral reply; 3) to consider the employee's answer if the employee has been granted an extension to answer (for example, if the employee has been ill or incapacitated); 4) to consider reasonable accommodation of a handicapping condition; 5) to consider positions to which the employee might be reassigned or reduced in grade (if required by agency procedures); or 6) to comply with a stay ordered by a member of the MSPB. (5 C.F.R. 432.105(a)(4)(i)(B) (1996))

If an agency believes that an extension of the advance notice period is necessary for a reason other than one of the six outlined above, it may request prior approval for such an extension from OPM. (5 C.F.R. 432.105(a)(4)(i)(C) (1996)

This regulation is designed to encourage managers to confront performance deficiencies promptly and to make timely decisions concerning problem employees, while also allowing the employee a full and fair opportunity to respond to the proposed action.

Employee Status During The Notice Period

No regulatory provision requires immediate removal from the work-site of an employee who performs unacceptably during the 30-day notice period. Thus, the employee should remain in a duty status until a decision on the adverse action is made. This makes a great deal of sense. The supervisor should keep in mind that a performance-based adverse action is legally and conceptually one that is not considered to be the fault of the employee.

The conclusion to be reached by the supervisor and the agency officials charged with the responsibility of deciding the adverse action is not whether the employee committed a wrong, but whether the employee failed to meet a performance standard in a critical element. It is simply a matter of whether the employee is doing his job, and thus from a legal point of view no stigma attaches to an employee who is removed from a position for performance reasons.

Of course, an employee who is about to lose a job, whether it is for performance or other reasons, will be traumatized and will feel stigmatized. Compassion and understanding are therefore important. The supervisor should avoid expressions of animosity or the development of adversarial positions in a performance adverse action. This may be difficult, since an employee who is the subject of a performance adverse action may take on an adversarial role. The supervisor should attempt to rise above this and approach the performance adverse action without moral judgment. The supervisor must simply evaluate whether the employee is adequately performing the job.

The Employee Is Entitled To Respond To The Agency's Adverse Action

The employee may respond to the agency's proposed action orally and in writing. The employee also is entitled to be represented by an attorney or other representative of his choosing.

If the employee raises the existence of a medical condition which may have contributed to his unacceptable performance, the agency must consider any medical evidence the employee submits to support this claim.

In cases where the employee submits medical evidence of a disability and has the requisite time of service under the Federal Employees' Retirement System (FERS) (18 months) or the Civil Service Retirement System (CSRS) (five years), the agency must provide the employee with information describing eligibility for and the procedure for applying to OPM for disability retirement. (5 C.F.R. 432.105 a)(4)(iv))

Demotion Or Removal Is At Agency s Discretion

The decision whether to demote or remove an employee whose performance is "unacceptable" is within the sole discretion of the agency, and the decision or penalty will not be reviewed by the MSPB. Thus, the Douglas factors discussed in Chapter 5 are not considered in determining the propriety of an agency's action in a performance case.

The Agency Must Issue Written Notice Of Its Decision

Once the agency has fully considered any evidence offered by the employee, it must issue the employee a written notice of its decision at or before the time the action becomes effective. The final decision in a performance adverse action must be made within 30 days after the end of the advance notice period. In arriving at its decision, the agency must consider any answer of the employee or his representative furnished in response to the agency's proposal. (5 C.F.R. 432.105(b) (1996))

The written notice must advise the employee of specific instances of unacceptable performance upon which the decision is based.

At a minimum, the decision to remove must be concurred in by an official in the agency who is higher than the proposing official, unless the proposing official is the agency head. (5 U.S.C. 4303(b)(1)(D)(ii)) Most agencies elect to have the decision proposed by a first or second level supervisor with the concurring decision made by the next higher level supervisor. The written decision must also inform the employee of any applicable appeal and/or grievance rights, such as how to appeal the action to the MSPB, how to seek arbitration if authorized by union contract, and/or how to file an EEO complaint if appropriate. (5 C.F.R. 432.105(b) (1996))

Early Retirement As An Alternative To A Performance Adverse Action

In cases where the agency has proposed a performance-based adverse action that will result in removal, the agency may inform an eligible employee that he may seek early retirement from the agency. To be eligible, the employee must have 20 years of government service and be age 50, or have 25 years of government service at any age. There is a 2% annual reduction for each year the annuitant is under 55.

This may be a particularly attractive alternative for an eligible employee, since the employee's permanent employment record will reflect that he has retired, rather than that he was involuntarily discharged.

A performance adverse action constitutes removal for a reason other than misconduct or delinquency, which permits employees to be eligible for early retirement. In order to offer this option to the employee, the agency must first ensure that the employee has the requisite years of service. (Law enforcement officers and others with early-out rights may be differently situated; the personnel office should be consulted.) Since the MSPB upholds

Four Myths Of The Performance Appraisal System

the vast majority of all performance cases that it reviews, the early retirement option is particularly attractive to eligible employees.

• Difficulty Connected with Removing a Non-Performing Employee

Many managers and supervisors harbor common misconceptions about the performance appraisal system.

For instance, some believe that it is difficult to fire an employee for poor performance or non-performance. In fact, the Civil Service Reform Act (CSRA) was designed to assist federal managers in removing non-performing employees from the federal workforce. The reason the MSPB so readily sustains the supervisor's assessment is that the CSRA places a lower standard of proof on an agency in an appeal of a performance-based adverse action. Cases involving misconduct require a higher standard of proof by an agency. While this may appear to be a mere legal technicality, it does in fact have a significant impact on an agency's ability to effect a performance-based adverse action. (See discussion in Chapter 8.)

• Documentation Required to Remove a Non-Performing Employee

A second misconception held by some supervisors is that firing an employee for poor performance may require more documentation than it is worth. The documentation necessary for taking a performance-based adverse action is based on the employee's work plan, required of all federal workers. From there, the agency documents a poor performer against the elements and standards already developed. Thus, while performance-based adverse actions require some documentation, that process is largely related to the work plan developed at the beginning of the appraisal cycle. As for the effort expended by an agency in documenting a performance action versus the value of removing a non-performer, an agency stands to benefit greatly, in terms of efficiency, by removing a non-performing employee who cannot be rehabilitated.

• Timing of Performance-Based Actions

Many supervisors incorrectly believe that performance actions may only be taken in conjunction with the employee's annual appraisal.

OPM regulations explicitly state that an agency may take action against an employee "at any time during the performance appraisal cycle" that the employee's performance is determined to be unacceptable. (5 C.F.R. 432.104) Supervisors need only satisfy any minimum period that might be required by the agency's internal plan.

• Effect of Prior High Ratings on Ability to Take a Performance Action

The fourth myth is that an agency cannot discharge an employee who received high performance ratings in previous years. Prior performance, however, *is not dispositive or even relevant in the agency's proof of a performance-based action,* where current performance is the only issue. In fact, as long as the agency has carefully complied with the procedures discussed in Chapters 8 through 10 for drafting valid performance standards and for managing unacceptable performance, the MSPB almost always agrees with a supervisor's assessment of an employee's poor performance without regard to the employee's prior record. The only realistic concern about previously high performance ratings would be in connection with an affirmative defense. (See Chapters 6, 13 and 19.)

Under such circumstances the agency need offer only the reasons for the differences in the ratings. In an affirmative defense the burden of proof is on the employee, not the agency. In general, affirmative defenses are not often successful. Therefore, the agency should not allow the fear of an affirmative defense to stand in the way of taking a good faith action when it is warranted, even if a poorly performing employee has received high ratings in earlier years.

Employee Entitled To Reasonable Period of Time To Prepare Response

The agency must provide the employee with a reasonable period of time to prepare a response to a proposed performance adverse action.

Most agencies provide an employee 8 to 16 hours of administrative leave for case preparation, although up to 40 hours could be reasonable, depending on the complexity of the issues and the forum in which the case is being considered.

For example, to prepare for an oral reply in an adverse action at the agency level, an employee may only require a few hours to consult with his representative and meet with agency officials. However, a complex case with significant documentation may require additional time.

Appeal To MSPB

An employee who is not serving a probationary period has the right to appeal a demotion or removal decision to the MSPB. Chapter 21 discusses the MSPB process in detail.

Considerations For A Performance-Based Adverse Action

- Draft performance standards which set forth objective criteria for the critical elements of the position so that the employee knows what he must do to earn a rating of "acceptable performance." The performance standards should measure each employee's level of performance as effectively, objectively, and completely as possible.

- Define unacceptable performance within the performance standards before any unacceptable performance occurs. In other words, give advance notice of what is expected.

- Communicate the performance standards to each employee and ensure that the employee understands the standards. Answer any questions the employee may have regarding his work plan. Document the meeting where performance standards are communicated to the employee.

- If an employee's performance is unacceptable, take immediate action by conducting frequent informal counseling. Keep a record of the counseling contacts with the employee. Do not wait for the performance rating period to end.
- Offer the employee a meaningful performance improvement period or plan (PIP).

- At the conclusion of the PIP, determine whether performance remains unacceptable by comparing the employee's actual performance during the PIP to the employee's written performance standards.

- If the employee's performance remains unacceptable, propose the adverse action. Rely only on the employee's performance within the preceding one year.

- Provide the employee 30-days notice, a right to respond, and a right to review the materials upon which the action is based. The notice period may be extended an extra 30 days under the regulations prescribed by the head of the agency. An additional extension may be given by the agency, and OPM approval may or may not be requested, depending upon the reason for the extension.

- Make decisions regarding demotion or removal within 30 days of the end of the notice period.

- Issue written notice of the decision to the employee at or before the time the action will be effective.

Checklist For Performance Adverse Action

✔	Draft objective performance standards.
✔	Define unacceptable performance in performance standards.
✔	Communicate performance standards to each employee.
✔	Conduct immediate, frequent and informal counseling for unacceptable performance.
✔	Provide a meaningful PIP.
✔	Evaluate performance at conclusion of PIP.
✔	Propose adverse action based upon unacceptable performance of preceding year.
✔	Provide 30 days notice and right to respond.
✔	Issue decisions within 30 days after notice period ends.
✔	Document all meetings.

How To Handle Cases That Contain Both Performance And Misconduct Issues

Cases That Contain Both Performance & Misconduct

The previous chapters have discussed the differences between performance and misconduct cases and the distinct processes which must be followed in handling each type of adverse action. In the course of a career a federal manager may encounter cases where the performance of a problem employee includes elements of both misconduct and poor performance.

When this occurs, the supervisor must choose whether to use the misconduct procedures discussed in Chapters 2 through 7 or the performance procedures highlighted in Chapters 8 through 11. The United States Court of Appeals for the Federal Circuit has held that an agency can, at its discretion, use either method; *see Lovshin v. Dep't. of the Navy,* 767 F.2d 826 (Fed. Cir. 1985), *cert. denied,* 475 U.S. 1111 (1986).

Distinctions Between Performance & Misconduct Cases

As discussed in Chapters 8 and 9, an employee's level of performance is determined by adherence to specific performance standards. Misconduct, which is ordinarily measured against an agency's rules of conduct (see Chapters 2 and 3), may also be established by reference to an employee's performance. For example, a deliberate act of non-adherence to a performance standard may constitute insubordination.

☑ CASE IN POINT

If a critical element of Jane's job requires her to operate a shuttle between two government buildings, the agency could initiate a performance adverse action against her if she drives the shuttle over the speed limit, or if she does not strictly adhere to the shuttle schedule.

In contrast, if Jane deliberately operates over the speed limit or intentionally ignores the schedule because she does not wish to follow her supervisor's instructions, a misconduct action might be justified; cf. Lovato v. Dep't. of Air Force, 48 M.S.P.R. 198 (1991).

In addition, serious one-time performance problems may justify a misconduct adverse action, even if the deficiency was not deliberate.

☑ CASE IN POINT

John works for the Federal Aviation Administration as an air traffic controller. His job description states that in routing the traffic of aircraft, his performance must always be "fully successful." This standard is attained by keeping aircraft adequately separated at all times. Although this is an absolute standard, such absolute standards are permissible where any deviation from the standard could result in risk to human life. If two airplanes nearly collide during John's shift due to his negligence, the agency may immediately initiate adverse action procedures to remove John from his position. The agency is not required to use the performance procedures, including the PIP, to remove or demote John. It can proceed with an action immediately using the misconduct procedure; cf. Giltner v. Dep't of Air Force, 39 M.S.P.R. 253 (1988).

A misconduct case at the Merit Systems Protection Board (MSPB) is evaluated by reference to the "efficiency of the service standard," as discussed in Chapters 2 and 3. A performance case, on the other hand, is always analyzed by reference to whether a performance standard in a critical element has been attained. The agency must prove a performance deficiency at the MSPB by "substantial evidence." In a misconduct case, the agency must prove the charge by the higher standard of "preponderance of the evidence." (5 C.F.R. 1201.56(a))

Use Of Misconduct System For Defective Performance Cases

In taking a performance adverse action, the agency is limited to relying upon evidence that is no more than one year old in evaluating the employee's performance. In addition, under the performance adverse action procedures, an employee must be given an opportunity to improve his performance. (5 C.F.R. 432.104-432.105(a)(3) (1996)) Where the agency has strong evidence of an employee's poor performance and some or all of the performance allegations are more than one year old, or where the agency believes allowing the employee to remain on the job during a performance improvement plan (PIP) could be potentially harmful to the agency, the agency may wish to initiate a misconduct case against the employee. This is particularly appropriate if the performance deficiency is serious, such as in cases where life or property are, or were, threatened by the employee's poor performance. In such instances, the performance standard, notice, and PIP requirements have not been and cannot be met, due to the passage of time, making a misconduct case the only remedy.

Before deciding whether to utilize the performance procedures, which allow the employee an opportunity to improve his performance during a PIP, or the misconduct procedures, which do not provide the employee with a PIP period, managers should be aware of several additional considerations.

First, in reviewing an agency's proposed action, the MSPB may mitigate actions taken under misconduct procedures, but will not mitigate actions taken under performance procedures. Thus, if the agency proposes to remove an employee under the misconduct procedures, the MSPB may determine that such a penalty is overly harsh in light of the employee's misconduct, and may mitigate the removal to a demotion, suspension, reprimand, or no penalty. In contrast, if the agency proposes to remove an employee under the performance procedures, the main issue is the employee's performance. Therefore, the MSPB will simply decide whether the employee should be remain in his current position, be removed, or be demoted. The MSPB will not, however, mitigate the proposed removal or demotion in a performance based action.

Second, before opting to proceed under the misconduct procedures, managers should be careful to ensure that the employee had notice of his performance standards, and that the agency is not attempting to circumvent the performance procedures by charging that the employee should have performed better than the standards communicated to him. If the employee did not have notice of his performance standards, the agency must proceed with the performance procedures, and place the employee on a PIP. The agency should not proceed under the misconduct procedures.

☑ **CASE IN POINT**

Sam is an electrician for the Department of the Navy and works in a Navy facility. Sam is expected to diligently and appropriately install electrical wire in certain Navy facilities. Sam is also expected to comply with applicable building codes. As a result of a routine inspection of Sam's work, the Navy discovers that Sam's work is substandard and does not comply with applicable building codes, creating a potential safety hazard. Sam's supervisor checks Sam's performance standards and notes that the performance standard concerning the adequacy of Sam's work fails to include a provision about complying with local building codes. In addition, the supervisor recalls that two years earlier Sam had a similar problem and needed to be counseled.

Under these circumstances, while Sam's performance standard does not refer specifically to compliance with the local building codes, and these standards were communicated to Sam more than a year ago, the agency could choose to process Sam's case under the misconduct procedures. The fact that Sam's poor performance creates a safety hazard would make the agency's use of misconduct procedures appropriate.

Since Sam was already on notice of what was expected of him, and the agency should be able to establish the existence of a building code and Sam's failure to comply with it, the agency could proceed against Sam using misconduct procedures instead of performance procedures. If the agency initiated an adverse action against Sam on the basis of misconduct procedures, it would be unnecessary for the agency to give Sam a notice of opportunity to improve, or to conform with other compliance procedures ordinarily required before initiating a performance adverse action; cf. Gende v. Dep't. of Justice, 35 M.S.P.R. 518 (1987).

Along these lines, in a misconduct adverse action where there is a record of a serious deficiency, such as negligent performance of duties, there is no requirement that the agency notify the employee of deficient performance; (*see Fairall v. Veterans Administration,* 844 F.2d 775, 776 (Fed. Cir. 1987). In *Fairall,* a medical technician made several errors in recording blood test results in a lab book which was sometimes consulted by doctors. The court stated that this was not simply a matter of performance deficiencies, but also a matter of "misconduct, neglect of duty, or malfeasance." The court further found that the employee's negligent acts "would destroy the confidence of doctors and staff in the reliability of laboratory reports." Thus, it was inappropriate to follow the employee performance procedural prerequisites before removing the employee.

Douglas Factor Rules ...

WHEN THE MISCONDUCT SYSTEM IS USED FOR PERFORMANCE CASES

The MSPB applies special rules concerning the *Douglas* factors when an agency uses the misconduct system to discipline an employee for what is essentially a performance problem. (See Chapter 5 for a complete discussion of the *Douglas* factors.)

The MSPB will mitigate a removal penalty when misconduct procedures are used if the agency has failed to provide an employee with an opportunity period or other notice of what is expected of the employee, unless the employee's non-performance is willful or concerns a matter of health or safety; *see Fairall v. Veterans Administration,* 33 M.S.P.R. 33, 39-47 (1987), *aff'd,* 844 F.2d 775 (Fed. Cir. 1987) (where an agency used misconduct procedures to effect an adverse action for poor performance).

The employee has no statutory right to an opportunity period when misconduct procedures are used, so the failure to provide one is relevant only to the appropriateness of the penalty. An agency should only use misconduct procedures in a case involving failure to perform when willfulness can be established, or a threat to health or safety can be demonstrated. Unless these standards can be met, the agency should not use misconduct procedures, and should process the case as a performance action using the procedures discussed above in Chapters 8 through 11. (As discussed in Chapter 11, the *Douglas* factors are not applied by the MSPB in a performance adverse action.)

Use Of Performance System For Misconduct Problems

An agency may consider using performance procedures against an employee for conduct problems under the following circumstances:

• The agency's evidence against the employee is not strong;

• The agency has satisfied the requirements of all performance procedures, including proper notice, clear performance standards and critical elements, and a reasonable PIP;

• The employee's conduct can be measured by applying the performance standard to show unacceptable performance in a critical element.

For example, a performance standard which states that the employee who deals with the public must treat citizens with dignity and respect is not met if the employee is disrespectful to those with whom he deals, and the supervisor often receives complaints. However, the supervisor may not have strong evidence of misconduct since the citizens who complained may not wish to provide statements, or testify. Thus while the disrespect is misconduct, it is also deficient performance, and the supervisor may wish to place the employee on a PIP, attempt to rehabilitate him, and only seek to remove the employee if he doesn't improve. Using the performance procedures should only require the supervisor's testimony in support of the appraisal. That evidence should be sufficient to constitute "substantial evidence" and support a performance action, although it would probably not be sufficient to constitute the "preponderance of the evidence" necessary to support a misconduct action.

• The employee demonstrates elements of both misconduct and poor performance.

For example, an employee who appears to be deliberately refusing to do his job is guilty of insubordination. The supervisor of such an employee may be able to show inadequate performance, but may lack adequate evidence to show that the employee deliberately failed to do the job. Under this circumstance, the supervisor should comply with the procedural requirements of a valid performance standard and PIP and then take action based on the employee's performance using the performance procedures discussed in Chapters 8 -11. The supervisor will not then need to prove the employee's intent by a preponderance of the evidence at an MSPB hearing, which is a requirement if charges of insubordination are brought.

Instead, the supervisor need only prove by substantial evidence that the employee failed to satisfy job expectations.

Using Performance Procedures For Misconduct	
1	Evidence of misconduct is not strong, particularly if the employee's intent must be proved by the agency.
2	Performance standards are clear.
3	The performance improvement plan has been completed.
4	The employee's conduct can be measured by application of the performance standard.
Examples: Discourteous conduct, insubordination, or failure to properly complete assignment.	

Whistleblowing Cases

When An Employee Charges That A Personnel Action (Or Non-Action) Is Reprisal For His Alleged Whistleblowing

Whistleblowing Cases

All federal employees who are whistleblowers are protected against unlawful reprisal.

The Burden Of Proof

WHEN AN EMPLOYEE CHARGES THAT A PERSONNEL ACTION (OR NON-ACTION) IS REPRISAL FOR HIS ALLEGED WHISTLEBLOWING

The word "whistleblowing" refers to an employee's disclosure or release of information which he believes: 1) shows that a law, rule, or regulation has been violated, or 2) shows evidence of gross mismanagement, an excessive waste of funds, an abuse of authority, or a considerable and specific danger to public health or safety. (5 U.S.C. 1213(a)(1)) Whistleblowing includes an employee's disclosure of this type of information to officials in his chain of command, to the Office of Special Counsel (OSC) or to the Inspector General of an agency. (An employee may also disclose this type of information to any other employee designated by the head of the agency to receive these disclosures.)

Under the Whistleblower Protection Act of 1989 (WPA), a federal statute, an employee who engages in whistleblowing is entitled to protection from adverse personnel actions based at least in part on the disclosures. Specifically, an employee may appeal a personnel action that the agency takes, proposes, threatens, or fails to take because of the employee's whistleblowing activities. (Whistleblower Reprisal is one of the prohibited personnel practices discussed in Chapter 6.) The employee will not benefit from whistleblower protection, however, where the employee's disclosure of information is specifically prohibited by law or is required to be kept secret in the interest of national defense or the management of foreign affairs. (5 U.S.C. 1213(a)(1))

All federal employees who are whistleblowers, as defined by the WPA, are protected against unlawful reprisal. A supervisor who retaliates against a whistleblower because of the whistleblowing activity does so at his peril. A supervisor should not feel paralyzed, however, when dealing with a whistleblower. In fact, a supervisor should deal with a whistleblower subordinate in the same manner as if the whistleblowing had not occurred.

A whistleblower who is also a problem employee can be effectively rehabilitated or disciplined without violating any reprisal laws, if the supervisor approaches the employee with the proper attitude and attention to job-related criteria. Time and again, the Merit Systems Protection Board (MSPB) has recognized that federal managers must be allowed to manage, and the Board will uphold properly documented and motivated personnel actions even against whistleblowers. This chapter explains what happens when whistleblower retaliation is alleged.

In whistleblowing cases an employee has the burden of proof to demonstrate that: 1) his alleged whistleblowing activity is the type of protected activity defined by the statute (as discussed in the preceding section); and 2) his whistleblowing activities were a "contributing factor" in the adverse personnel action taken or proposed against him. (5 U.S.C. 1214(b)(4)(B)(i)) The employee must prove his case by a preponderance of the evidence. Thus, in order to prevail under this burden of proof, the employee must demonstrate that it is more likely true than untrue that events occurred as he describes them, and retaliation occurred.

The agency will win the case and the manager's decision will be upheld, if it demonstrates by clear and convincing evidence that it would have taken (or not taken, as the case may be) the same personnel action against the employee even if the whistleblowing had not occurred. (5 U.S.C. 1214(b)(4)(B)(ii)) Clear and convincing evidence is a higher, more demanding standard of proof than preponderance of the evidence. Clear and convincing evidence means that the deciding official, judge, or panel must be convinced rather than merely persuaded, that the agency's version of any disputed fact is correct.

Processing A Whistleblowing Case

Certain personnel actions which an employee may claim were taken or not taken as reprisal for whistleblowing may be appealed by the employee directly to the MSPB. (5 U.S.C. 1221(a))

For example, if the employee is subjected to a removal, demotion, or suspension of 15 days or more, he may appeal directly to the MSPB if he believes the action was reprisal for his whistleblowing. (5 C.F.R. 1201.3)

If the employee has suffered a personnel action for which he has no right of appeal directly to the MSPB under any law, rule or regulation, the employee must first seek corrective action from the OSC if he believes that the agency's adverse action is based on retaliation for whistleblowing activities. (5 U.S.C. 1214 (a)(3))

Examples of the types of personnel actions not directly appealable to MSPB are suspensions of less than fifteen (15) days, reassignments, details, reprimands, poor job appraisals, and certain training decisions. If the OSC, after considering the matter, decides that the agency's action was not justified, it will seek reversal of the agency's action and appropriate relief for the employee from the MSPB. For example, if the employee was wrongfully reassigned, OSC will ask the MSPB to reinstate the employee to the employee's original job. The Special Counsel may also request that the MSPB impose discipline against a federal manager if the manager is found to have engaged in whistleblower reprisal.

If the Special Counsel concludes, however, that the agency was justified in taking its action and that the action was not taken in reprisal for whistleblowing activity, the Special Counsel will so advise the employee, who may then individually appeal his case to the MSPB. This type of proceeding is known as an Individual Right of Action appeal.

The individual right of action (IRA) appeal applies only to allegations of whistleblower reprisal and does not extend the MSPB appeal right to any other type of prohibited personnel practice, or any other type of reprisal, such as retaliation for filing an EEO complaint; *see Spruill v. MSPB*, 978 F.2d 679 (Fed. Cir. 1992).

☑ CASE IN POINT

The General Services Administration gave Clarence a "minimally satisfactory" rating on a critical element on his annual performance appraisal. Clarence believes that the agency gave him the "minimally satisfactory" rating due to his whistleblowing activities. Since a performance evaluation cannot be directly appealed to the MSPB, Clarence must first seek corrective action from the Special Counsel before he files an appeal with the MSPB. Clarence may appeal the evaluation to the MSPB only after the Special Counsel completes its proceedings. If Clarence has received no response from the Special Counsel within 120 days after he files his request, he may file his own appeal with the MSPB any time after the 120 days have passed. (5 C.F.R. 1209.2(b)(1)); cf. Weber v. Dep't. of Army, 47 M.S.P.R. 130 (1991).

☑ CASE IN POINT

The Department of Transportation proposes to suspend Marcie for 15 days. Marcie believes that the agency has proposed her suspension because of her whistleblowing activities. Because a suspension of more than 14 days may be directly appealed to the MSPB, Marcie may choose to file an appeal with the MSPB without first seeking corrective action from the Special Counsel. However, if she desires to seek corrective action from the Special Counsel, Marcie may do so. Marcie may then later file an appeal to the MSPB if the Special Counsel supports the agency's proposed suspension. However, if she elects to seek corrective action from OSC, Marcie cannot file an appeal with the MSPB until after exhausting her remedies with the OSC. (5 C.F.R. 1209.2(b)(2)); cf. Gergick v. GSA, 49 M.S.P.R. 384 (1991); see also, Hornby v. Dep't of Navy, 61 M.S.P.R. 246 (1994).

Personnel Actions for Which Whistleblower Reprisal May be Appealed Directly to the MSPB
◆   Removals for misconduct or poor performance.
◆   Demotions for misconduct or poor performance.
◆   Suspensions of more than 14 days.

Personnel Actions Which Must be Referred to the Office of Special Counsel Before Being Appealed to the MSPB
◆   Appointments.
◆   Promotions.
◆   Re-employment.
◆   Performance appraisals.
◆   Decisions concerning education or training expected to lead to appointments, promotions, or other personnel actions.
◆   Changes in duties inconsistent with the employee's salary or grade level.

Time Periods For Filing A Whistleblowing Appeal

Unless the agency's adverse personnel action is directly appealable to the MSPB (see also page 162), the employee must file a whistleblowing complaint with the Special Counsel before he can appeal the personnel action to the MSPB. If the OSC notifies the employee that it has terminated its investigation of the employee's allegations, the employee must file an appeal with the MSPB no more than 60 days after the Special Counsel issues its written notification to the employee. (5 U.S.C. 1214(a)(3)(A)(i) and (ii)) If the employee receives no response from the Special Counsel within 120 days of the date he files his request for corrective action, the employee may file an appeal to the MSPB anytime after 120 days have passed. (5 U.S.C. 1214(a)(3)(B)) Although the statute allows only 60 days in which to appeal a whistleblower complaint following termination of the Special Counsel's investigation, it is now common practice by the OSC to notify complainants that they have 65 days to appeal to MSPB under the regulations interpreting the statute. This discrepancy is not easily explained, and employees pursuing whistleblower complaints probably should not exceed the statutory 60-day period unless absolutely necessary.

Employee May Seek A "Stay"

A "stay" or freeze means the agency's action will not become effective until after the Board has issued a decision in the employee's case.

At any time prior to the close of discovery in an MSPB appeal, the employee may request that the Board "stay," or freeze, the agency's adverse action. (5 C.F.R. 1209.8(a)) This means that the agency's action will not become effective until after the Board has issued a decision in the employee's case. An employee whose case is pending at OSC may ask the Special Counsel to seek a stay on his behalf.

☑ CASE IN POINT

The Customs Service proposes to terminate Bob from his job effective June 1st. Bob believes that the Customs Service is terminating him in retaliation for his disclosure of his supervisor's illegal activities. On June 2nd, Bob files an appeal to the MSPB. Bob's hearing at the MSPB will not begin until August 1st. Bob may wish to file a request for a stay of the Customs Service's action before, simultaneous with, or after he files his appeal on June 2nd. If the request is granted, the Customs Service may not terminate Bob until after the MSPB reaches a decision in the case. Thus, Bob will remain employed through at least the month of July, whereas he would have been terminated effective June 1st if he had not filed a request for the stay. (5 C.F.R. 1209.2(b)(3)); cf. Gergick v. GSA, 43 M.S.P.R. 651 (1990).

Processing For Obtaining A Stay Because of Whistleblower Reprisal

Agency decision to remove employee.

Request for stay filed with MSPB within 20 days after removal effected, but not later than date set for close of discovery when an MSPB appeal has already been filed.

10 days

MSPB administrative judge issues decision on Stay.	20 days from date of MSPB decision.	File MSPB appeal on removal if not already filed.

The MSPB has detailed regulations concerning the proper procedures for filing a request for a stay, including where the request should be filed and what it should contain. (5 C.F.R. 1209.8 and 1209.9) The agency is entitled to file a response to the employee's stay request in which it may indicate whether the grant of a stay would result in extreme hardship to the agency. The agency also must set forth in its response an argument addressing whether there is a substantial likelihood that the appellant will prevail on the merits of his appeal and may provide supporting documentation. (5 C.F.R. 1209.9(c))

Although not required to do so, the MSPB administrative judge may hold a hearing on the stay request. The judge must issue a ruling on the stay request within ten (10) days after the employee files the request with the proper MSPB regional office. (5 C.F.R. 1209.10) In making his decision, the judge must make a preliminary ruling on whether there is a substantial likelihood that the employee will win his appeal of the agency's adverse action.

If the employee files a request for a stay with the Board before the employee files an appeal, he must file an appeal within 30 days after the date the MSPB issues an order ruling on the stay request. (5 C.F.R. 1209.5(c)) If the employee misses this deadline, the MSPB may terminate any stay it has granted unless the employee can show a good reason for the delay.

Prosecution For Whistleblower Reprisal

The immediate concern of a supervisor in a whistleblower case is the possibility that he may be prosecuted for alleged retaliation against the whistleblower. As mentioned previously, whistleblower reprisal is a prohibited personnel practice and is subject to investigation by the OSC and prosecution by the Special Counsel before the MSPB. Possible penalties for a supervisor range from debarment from federal employment to removal, suspension, demotion, reprimand, and a fine.

One of the significant factors for a supervisor to remember in a whistleblower case is that the employee maintains more control over the outcome of the case than in a traditional appeal. A decision by the MSPB contrary to the supervisor's contentions on a whistleblower reprisal issue could be referred to the OSC and might be closely scrutinized by that Office for possible disciplinary action or prosecution.

Despite this risk, the supervisor who acts carefully, and with the proper motivation, should not fear prosecution for whistleblower reprisal. Further, adverse personnel actions that have already been started or for which planning has been substantially completed when the whistleblowing starts cannot constitute reprisal.

Thus, careful documentation will help establish a defense in the event that an allegation of whistleblower reprisal is raised. A supervisor could also avoid liability by showing that the alleged retaliatory personnel action was ordered by higher authority or required to be effected by rules and regulations.

Analyzing A Whistleblower Reprisal Case

It is significant that an employee need only demonstrate that the whistle-blowing was a contributing factor to a personnel action.

The above discussion outlines the manner in which a whistleblower reprisal case is processed. In analyzing the whistleblower reprisal case, essentially, the employee has to establish that the protected disclosure was a contributing factor in the decision to take the personnel action. The agency will prevail by proving with clear and convincing evidence that it would have taken the action anyway. Under the Whistleblower Protection Act of 1989, as originally interpreted by the MSPB, an employee could utilize circumstantial evidence to prove that protected disclosures were a contributing factor in an adverse personnel action. However, the U.S. Court of Appeals for the Federal Circuit rejected this interpretation in *Clark v. Dep't of Army,* 997 F.2d 1466 (Fed. Cir. 1993). In that case, the Court of Appeals held that facts tending to show a temporal connection between a protected disclosure and a personnel action did not necessarily establish a *prima facie* case of whistleblower reprisal.

In 1994, however, in direct response to the decision of the Federal Circuit in *Clark,* Congress unequivocally stated that if the employee shows a closeness in time between engaging in protected activity and the adverse personnel action, the employee will establish that the whistleblowing activity was a contributing factor in the personnel action. (5 U.S.C. 1221 (e)(1)(B))

It is significant that an employee need only demonstrate that the whistleblowing was a contributing factor. Thus, if an employee complains to an Inspector General about alleged illegal activity and shortly thereafter the employee experiences some unexplained and unexpected personnel action, an inference of reprisal will exist. The agency will be required to rebut by clear and convincing evidence.

The previous law on establishing whistleblower reprisal and the current law on all other types of reprisal require an employee to show that the reprisal was a significant factor in the personnel action, a higher standard than contributing factor; *see Special Counsel v. Eidmann,* 976 F.2d 1400 (Fed. Cir. 1992). In *Eidmann,* the Federal Circuit decided that the higher significant factor standard currently applies to whistleblower reprisal prosecution cases brought against an alleged retaliating manager by the OSC or the supervisor's agency.

Nature Of Protected Disclosures

In order for a whistleblower to claim protection under the WPA, he must not only make a disclosure, but he must also reasonably believe at the time of his disclosures, that he is disclosing evidence of illegal or improper activity covered by the WPA. While there is no requirement that an employee make disclosures while acting in good faith, an employee who does not have an objectively reasonable belief that he is disclosing such activity does not enjoy whistleblower protection; *see, e.g., Horton v. Dep't of Navy,* 66 F.3d 279, 282-83 (Fed. Cir. 1995).

Similarly, the MSPB has held that an employee who raises issues of regulatory violations and the like in pursuing a personal grievance, such as a discrimination complaint, administrative grievance, unfair labor practice charge, or even an MSPB appeal, is not a protected whistleblower entitled to bring a claim of whistleblower reprisal under 5 U.S.C. 2302(b)(8); *see Spruill v. MSPB*, 978 F.2d 679 (Fed. Cir. 1992); *William v. Dep't. of Defense*, 46 M.S.P.R. 549 (1991), *vac'd. on other grounds*, 47 M.S.P.R. 461 (1991); *Ruffin v. Dep't. of the Army*, 48 M.S.P.R. 74 (1991); *Crist v. Dep't. of the Navy*, 50 M.S.P.R. 35 (1991); *Coffer v. Dep't. of the Navy*, 50 M.S.P.R. 54 (1991). Notably however, a claim for worker's compensation may constitute whistleblowing for purposes of the WPA; *see Von Kelsch v. Dep't. of Labor*, 59 M.S.P.R. 503 (1993).

Also, an employee who submits false information or who lies deliberately in a whistleblower claim is likely to not have a reasonable belief that the information they have disclosed is evidence of wrongdoing as defined by the WPA, and will probably not enjoy the protection of the WPA.

OSC Investigations

If a manager or supervisor becomes the target of an investigation by the OSC and is directed to attend an interview with an OSC investigator, he should immediately seek the assistance of the General Counsel's Office and ask for representation by an attorney from that office. If this request is denied, the agency should be requested to pay for a private attorney. The Comptroller General has ruled that an agency may do so, although it is not required to do so. (67 Comp. Gen. 37 (1987)) If the agency refuses, the supervisor should seriously consider paying for a private attorney to represent him at the interview. If the manager or supervisor has a professional liability insurance policy, it is also advisable to contact the insurer under the terms of that policy at that time. The OSC investigators are aggressive and are seeking information from a supervisor which can be used against him in any subsequent action they may decide to bring. OSC interviews or investigations should not be taken lightly. A career may be at stake.

Discrimination And The Federal Equal Employment Opportunity System

Discrimination And The Federal EEO System

The anti-discrimination laws which control the federal workplace are designed to provide equal opportunities for all employees and applicants for employment without regard to their race, color, religion, sex, national origin, age or handicapping condition. These same laws provide a mechanism for administrative adjudication of discrimination complaints within the employee's or applicant's agency. In situations where an employee believes that the agency has discriminated against him, these procedures also allow the employee to seek relief from the Equal Employment Opportunity Commission (EEOC).

The EEOC supervises the employment practices of agencies in order to protect the rights of individuals working for the federal government and to ensure that discrimination does not occur. The EEOC is authorized to review allegations of discrimination from federal employees, and where appropriate, order relief. (29 C.F.R. Part 1614) Among other things, the EEOC may require an agency to stop discrimination against an employee and award relief such as reinstatement, pain and suffering, back pay, and attorney fees. In cases where the agency does not stop discrimination voluntarily or after ordered to do so by the EEOC, the employee may sue the agency in federal district court.

Maintaining a discrimination-free work environment is an important part of every supervisor's job. Most agencies have critical elements that require effective functioning with respect to EEO laws and the EEO system. Thus, a supervisor should be familiar with anti-discrimination laws and with the administrative complaint-filing process in the federal government. This chapter briefly explains how the EEO system works in the federal government. The procedures discussed in this chapter may be found at 29 C.F.R. Parts 1613 and 1614.

The Agency's Role In Carrying Out EEO Programs

Federal law requires the head of each federal agency to personally establish and carry out an affirmative action program, so that EEO policies are used in every aspect of work throughout the agency. In establishing this goal, it is expected that the head of each agency will take every possible step to bring EEO principles to the day-to-day functions of the agency. For example, the agency should acknowledge employees who demonstrate superior accomplishment in equal employment opportunities. The agency is also expected to provide counseling for employees and applicants who believe that they have been the victims of discrimination. In such cases, the agency's goal is to quickly resolve any complaints on an informal basis in a fair and impartial manner or, if necessary, provide a process for employees to pursue their complaints administratively. (29 C.F.R. 1614.102)

Pre-Complaint Processing And The EEO Counselor

The EEO complaint-filing process begins when an employee brings an allegation of discrimination on the basis of race, color, religion, sex, national origin, age or handicapping condition to an EEO counselor. (29 C.F.R. 1614.105)

At this initial step in the EEO process, the goal is to resolve the complaint with the assistance of an EEO counselor.

The EEO counselor's job is to obtain details about the employee's complaint and to counsel the employee about the issues he has raised. The EEO counselor should keep a record of the counseling which summarizes his activities, including the counselor's advice both to the employee and to the agency.

The EEO complaint-filing process has strict time limitations. An employee must contact an EEO counselor within 45 days of the discriminatory event being complained of or the agency has no obligation to process the complaint. However, the agency may extend this deadline if the complainant provides satisfactory reasons for not meeting the filing deadline; (29 C.F.R. 1614.105(a)(2)); *see Jarrell v. U.S. Postal Service,* 753 F.2d 1088 (D.C. Cir. 1985); *Oaxaca v. Roscoe,* 641 F.2d 386 (5th Cir. 1981); *Cooper v. Bell,* 628 F.2d 1208 (9th Cir. 1980).

> The EEO complaint-filing process has strict time limitations.

☑ CASE IN POINT

Elizabeth feels that she was discriminated against on the basis of her sex when she learned that she was not selected for a promotion and a less-qualified male was selected for the position. Elizabeth has never filed an EEO complaint before and is unaware that she is required to contact a counselor within 45 days of learning that she was not selected for the position. No EEO posters in the area where Elizabeth works provide this information.

Elizabeth contacts a counselor within 49 days. The agency may waive the 45-day filing time limit in this case, if it is satisfied that Elizabeth was not aware of the time limits and that this lack of knowledge was not her fault (e.g., inattention to EEO posters). The situation could be different if EEO posters had been displayed in Elizabeth's work area, but she never looked at them; cf. Morton v. Dep't. of Treasury, 44 M.S.P.R. 416 (1990).

It is illegal for the agency to interfere with the EEO counselor's duties in any manner throughout the EEO process. (29 C.F.R. 1614.102(b)(5)) A supervisor should consider allegations of discrimination raised in the EEO counseling stage to be serious matters. Compliance with this stage in the EEO process is a mandatory requirement for an employee before he can file a formal complaint, but it is also an opportunity for the agency to explain the basis of actions to the aggrieved employee, clear up misunderstandings between supervisors and employees, and perhaps informally resolve a potential dispute. Often an employee's EEO complaint results from a lack of information or a misunderstanding about why a particular action was taken.

> It is illegal to interfere with the EEO counselor's duties in any manner throughout the EEO process.

Many agencies successfully use the counseling stage to communicate with employees the reasons for management actions and thereby reduce the number of formal EEO complaints filed. For this reason, a supervisor should be candid with EEO counselors and explain the nondiscriminatory reasons for the agency's action.

> Supervisors should seriously consider any proposals by the EEO counselor to resolve EEO complaints at the informal stage.

Effective communication with the employee at this stage will aid in preventing the filing of a formal complaint, as well as avoid the imposition of additional expense and effort by the agency. Supervisors should also seriously consider any proposals discussed by the EEO counselor to resolve EEO complaints at the informal stage.

If informal resolution of the complaint is not accomplished, the EEO counselor must conduct a final interview with the complainant no more than 30 days after the employee brings his problem to the attention of the EEO counselor. The 30-day limit on counseling may be extended. Where the agency has an established dispute resolution procedure (such as mediation), the pre-complaint processing may continue for an additional 60 days. The EEO counselor must submit a written report of counseling within 15 days, if the complainant agrees to participate. In the absence of a dispute resolution procedure, the complainant may agree to an additional 60 day extension to pursue a resolution.

Once the 30-day or 90-day deadline for counseling or dispute resolution arrives, the EEO counselor must notify the complainant in writing that the complainant has only 15 days in which to file a formal discrimination complaint. (29 C.F.R. 1614.106(b))

If the complainant has retained an attorney or other representative, he must notify the agency and provide the identity of his representative to the agency at this point in the process. Unless the employee files a formal complaint against the agency, the EEO counselor is not permitted to reveal the employee's identity without permission from the complainant to do so. Most employees grant this permission.

Filing And Processing A Formal EEO Complaint

As noted previously, if an employee decides to file a formal EEO complaint against the agency, he must do so within 15 days of final counseling. An employee may also file a formal complaint if counseling has continued for more than 30 days and the complaint is still unresolved. (29 C.F.R. 1614.105(d))

☑ CASE IN POINT

Bob went for EEO counseling about a claim of race discrimination on November 1st. By December 5th no resolution has been reached in his case, and the counselor has not given him a final interview letter. Because more than 30 days have passed since he initiated EEO counseling, Bob may file a formal EEO complaint if he wishes, without waiting for the final interview.

Alternatively, Bob can wait for the final interview and, at that point, he will have 15 days in which to file a formal EEO complaint; cf. Baxter v. Dep't. of Army, 45 M.S.P.R. 663 (1990).

As with the deadline for initially contacting an EEO counselor, the agency may extend the formal complaint filing deadlines if: 1) the employee demonstrates to the agency that he did not know about the deadlines, or 2) the employee provides any other reason the agency considers satisfactory.

The employee may file the formal complaint with the head of the agency, the agency's Director of Equal Employment Opportunity, the head of the field installation where the employee works, or any other person designated by the agency to receive EEO complaints. The notice of final interview will identify these individuals and provide filing addresses.

Assuming that the employee meets all deadlines and files the complaint with the correct person within the agency, the agency must notify the employee in writing that it has received the complaint. This notice or a subsequent one should include a statement regarding what allegations have been accepted by the agency for processing. The agency must also notify the employee that he has the right to file an action in court and the time limits for filing a court action. The agency should provide the employee a reasonable amount of official time to prepare his formal complaint. Similarly, if the employee's representative is also an agency employee, the agency should permit the representative to have a reasonable amount of official time to prepare the complaint. However, the agency is not required to change work schedules, pay overtime wages, or pay travel expenses to assist the employee in his choice of representative. Nor is the agency required to make these adjustments for the sole purpose of allowing the employee to confer with his representative.

If the employee and his representative are both authorized or required by the agency or the EEOC to be present during counseling, the investigation, or hearing stages of the complaint process, the employee and representative (if he is an agency employee and otherwise in a pay status) should be on official time. (29 C.F.R. 1614.605(b))

> The agency should provide the employee a reasonable amount of official time to prepare his formal complaint.

Rejection Or Cancellation Of Complaint

If the agency head or his designee determines that it is appropriate to cancel or reject the employee's complaint or portions thereof, the agency must notify the employee and his representative, if any, in writing. The agency's letter should inform the employee of his right to appeal the agency's decision to the EEOC or to court and should provide the appropriate filing time limits. A formal EEO complaint may be rejected for a reason such as untimeliness, and cancelled if, for example, 180 days have passed without completion of the investigation and the employee files a court action.

In that situation, the agency may cancel the administrative action so that it will not have to process both the administrative action and defend against the court action at the same time. The agency may also cancel an EEO complaint if the employee rejects a certified offer of full relief offered by the agency as a means of resolving his complaint. (29 C.F.R. 1614.107(h))

Investigation

The EEO investigator has the authority to investigate all aspects of the discrimination complaint.

☑ **CASE IN POINT**

Virgil filed an EEO complaint with his agency alleging that he was discriminated against on the basis of his sex when he was denied a temporary assignment to act in a position in which he would gain supervisory skills, enabling him to be more competitive for promotion opportunities. Virgil is represented by an attorney and has incurred about $580 in attorney's fees in the administrative process.

If the agency makes a settlement offer to Virgil which includes a similar position (assuming there is no difference in salary between this temporary assignment and Virgil's regular job) and payment of his attorney's fees, and Virgil refuses this offer, the agency may cancel the complaint under 29 C.F.R. 1614.107(h). In order to comply with the requirements of the EEO regulations, this offer must be certified as an offer of "full relief" by either the Director of the agency's Equal Employment Opportunity program or by a designee who reports to that Director; cf. Gardner v. Gartman, 880 F.2d 797 (4th Cir. 1989).

If the employee's formal complaint is accepted, the EEO office should immediately begin an investigation of the matters alleged in the complaint. The investigator should not be a person who works directly under the head of the section of the agency in which the employee's complaint arose. Many agencies contract with private consultants who conduct the investigation on behalf of the agency.

The EEO investigator has the authority to investigate all aspects of the discrimination complaint. This means that the investigator may require agency employees to cooperate with him in conducting the investigation, including such things as providing affidavits about their personal knowledge of events. The EEO investigator may also require agency officials to provide documents that are relevant to the issues raised in the EEO complaint. For example, if the allegations raised in the complaint relate to a promotion, the EEO investigator may require production of the promotion documents used in the selection process. The EEO investigation includes a thorough review of the circumstances surrounding the alleged discrimination. The EEO investigator should study the treatment of members of the employee's group, as identified in his complaint, compared to the treatment of other groups in the employee's division. (29 C.F.R. 1614.108)

☑ **CASE IN POINT**

Juanita, a Hispanic female employee, files a discrimination complaint alleging that her agency discriminates against Hispanic employees in making promotions. The investigator should examine statistics demonstrating how the agency treats its Hispanic employees as compared with employees of other nationalities. The investigation may uncover evidence of discrimination if it reveals that the agency has a pattern of promoting only non-Hispanic employees, even in cases where Hispanic employees are as qualified as or better qualified than other employees who were promoted; cf. Haine v. Dep't. of Navy, 41 M.S.P.R. 462 (1989).

The EEO investigator is responsible for creating an investigative file, which includes all of the information gathered in the course of the investigation. The EEO investigator is also responsible for producing a "Report of Investigation, (ROI)" which is a summary of the objective factual findings of the investigator. This information is used by the agency as a basis for the agency's proposed disposition of the EEO complaint. This part of the complaint process is explained further in this chapter.

The investigation ordinarily must be completed within 180 days. However, the investigation period may be extended an additional 90 days only by written agreement between the agency and the complainant. (29 C.F.R. 1614.108(e) The agency may be required to pay the costs of the complainant's discovery at a hearing before an EEOC administrative judge, if the complainant can show the discovery was needed because of the agency's failure to timely or adequately investigate the allegations of discrimination. (EEO MD-110, Chapter 6, III E) Once the investigation is completed, the complainant has the option of requesting a formal hearing before an administrative judge or requesting a final agency decision based on the investigation. (29 C.F.R. 1614.108(f)

Rights Of The Agency Official Accused Of Discrimination

Until recently, the agency official against whom a complaint of discrimination was made had rights by virtue of his status as an "alleged discriminating official" or ADO. These included the right to be told the specific charges, to be provided with a copy of the complainant's affidavit, and to be represented by an attorney during the interview with the EEO investigator.

The EEOC has revised its complaint process handbook and now considers ADOs to be in the same category as other federal employee witnesses; (see EEO MD-110, Chapter 5, VII A) Thus, the official position taken by the EEOC is that ADOs have the same rights as any other employee witness and thus must cooperate in the investigation without knowledge of the specific allegations in the complaint and without representation by an attorney. However, managers should insist on having such information before responding to specific charges against them. Notably, managers may be subjected to discipline if found liable for intentional discrimination against other employees. Under these circumstances, a manager should be entitled to know something about the charges before being expected to respond to them. In any event, as a practical matter, it will be necessary for the EEO counselor and investigator to explain the basis of a complaint to some extent in order to investigate and try to resolve it.

Along with the EEOC's change in position on the rights of agency officials accused of discrimination, it has deleted the term and concept of an "ADO." Many federal agencies have replaced the term with "Responsible Management Officials."

Certified Offer Of Full Relief

If an agency decides to resolve an EEO complaint before (or after) a determination is made as to whether discrimination actually occurred, the agency may offer a complainant "full relief." (29 C.F.R. 1614.107(h)) The full relief offer must be certified by the agency's EEO Director or Chief Legal Officer, or a designee who reports directly to one of them, and must allow the complainant 30 days to accept or reject the offer. The offer must be made prior to the issuance of a notification that the agency's investigation has been completed, and therefore it must also precede any hearing in the matter.

The offer of full relief must provide to the complainant all the relief the complainant would have received had he or she prevailed in the case. If it does, and the complainant rejects the offer, then the complaint may be dismissed by a final decision of the agency. The complainant may appeal the dismissal to the EEOC or file suit in federal district court. (29 C.F.R. 1614.110; 29 C.F.R. Part 1614, Subpart D)

Hearing

Though closed to the public, an EEOC hearing is similar to a courtroom trial in many respects.

After the EEO investigation has been completed, the complainant may request either a final agency decision or a hearing before an EEOC administrative judge.

An EEOC hearing is similar to a courtroom trial in many respects, but it is closed to the public. The hearing is recorded by a court reporter, and each side has the opportunity to present witnesses and submit exhibits to supplement the contents of the Investigative File.

After the administrative judge considers all of the evidence presented by the agency and the employee, the administrative judge will issue a recommended decision within 180 days from the date the EEOC received the hearing request. In this decision, the administrative judge will state whether he believes the agency has wronged the employee and, if so, what steps the agency should take to correct the problem. The administrative judge may also discuss the general environment at the agency, which led the employee to file the complaint. (29 C.F.R. 1614.109)

The law now allows an administrative judge to award not only such remedies as reinstatement and back pay to victims of discrimination, but also compensatory damages, which would include medical expenses, as well as pain and suffering damages, up to a total of $300,000; *see Jackson v. Runyon,* EEOC No. 01923399 (November 12, 1992).

A supervisor who is called as a witness at an EEOC hearing should review Chapter 21 or check out the December 1996 issue of *The Federal Manager's Edge* for helpful hints in testifying at the hearing.

Final Agency Decision

The administrative judge forwards the recommended decision to the agency, along with the hearing transcript and any additional exhibits admitted into the record at the hearing. This decision becomes the final decision of the agency within 60 days, unless the agency issues its own final decision within that time period. The final agency decision may accept, reject or modify the recommended decision. However, if the agency rejects or modifies the administrative judge's recommended decision, the agency must explain its specific reasons for doing so. In cases where there was no hearing and no recommended decision, the final agency decision must contain the agency's findings, analysis and decision in the case.

If the final agency decision is against the employee, the agency should notify the employee in the decision of his right to file an appeal with the EEOC or in court, and provide the time limits for filing an appeal or court action. (29 C.F.R. 1614.110)

Appeal To The EEOC

If an employee is dissatisfied with a final agency decision on the merits of his complaint or on a procedural matter, such as cancellation of a complaint for untimeliness, he may appeal it to the EEOC, Office of Federal Operations (formerly the Office of Review and Appeals), P.O. Box 19848, Washington, D.C. 20036. The Office of Federal Operations has authority to review the record generated in a complaint, including the EEO complaint file and the record of proceedings if a hearing was conducted on the complaint, and issue a final administrative decision. (29 C.F.R. 1614.403)

Either the agency or the employee may ask the EEOC to reopen and reconsider its decision on an appeal, and an employee who is dissatisfied with the EEOC's decision may seek relief in federal district court. (29 C.F.R. 1614.408; 42 U.S.C. 2000e-16(c)) However, the agency has no recourse in federal district court if the EEOC issues a decision in favor of the employee, and any corrective action ordered by the EEOC is binding upon the agency and enforceable in court. (29 C.F.R. 1614.504)

Burdens Of Proof In Discrimination Cases

The same burdens of proof apply to allegations of discrimination, whether the case is being adjudicated before a court or before an administrative judge from the EEOC.

The employee carries the initial burden of establishing what is called a *prima facie* case of discrimination based upon sex, race, religion, color, age, or national origin. (See Chapter 16 for a discussion on handicap discrimination.) This means that the employee must come forward with evidence of actions by the employer that, if not otherwise explained, would imply discrimination. Once the employee meets this burden, the employer is then required to articulate a legitimate nondiscriminatory reason for its actions. This burden is only to

Chapter 14

The employee bears the burden of proving intentional discrimination by a preponderance of the evidence.

produce or state a valid reason for the actions taken. The employer need not persuade the trier of fact that the reason articulated was the true reason for the action. Once the employer gives a reason for the challenged action, the employee then has the burden of establishing that the reason provided by the employer is merely pretextual, or not the true reason for the action taken. It is important to remember that the employee bears the burden of proving intentional discrimination by a preponderance of the evidence; *see McDonnell Douglas Corp. v. Green,* 411 U.S. 792 (1973); *Texas Dep't. of Community Affairs v. Burdine,* 450 U.S. 248 (1981). This burden is difficult to carry. The Supreme Court recently ruled that showing the employee's reason is not believable or is actually contrived does not necessarily establish discrimination. The employee must show that the action was discriminatory in nature; *St. Mary's Center v. Hicks,* 113 S.Ct. 2742 (1993).

Regarding religious discrimination, the EEOC requires that employers make reasonable accommodations for the religious needs of their employees. (29 C.F.R. 1605.2(b)) Thus, as part of a *prima facie* case of religious discrimination, the employee must establish that he advised the employer both of his religious needs and of the need for reasonable accommodation. The burden then shifts to the employer to demonstrate that it was unable to provide the accommodation sought without undue hardship; *see Ansonia Board of Education v. Philbrook,* 479 U.S. 60 (1986); *Redmond v. GAF Corporation,* 574 F.2d 897 (7th Cir. 1978).

Allegations Of Reprisal

Reprisal refers to an allegation that agency action was taken because an employee exercised his right to engage in protected activity, such as filing a prior EEO complaint. The burden of proof in a case of reprisal differs slightly from the burden of proof of other allegations of discrimination. The employee is required to establish that he engaged in a protected activity, demonstrate the individual taking the adverse personnel action was aware of the protected activity, and prove a nexus or connection between the protected activity and the personnel action alleged to be retaliatory.

The employer's defense is essentially the same as with other allegations of discrimination in that the employer meets its burden by articulating a legitimate, nondiscriminatory reason for the actions taken; *see Waddell v. Small Tube Products, Inc.,* 799 F.2d 69 (3d Cir. 1986); *Ruggles v. California Polytechnic State University,* 797 F.2d 782 (9th Cir. 1986); *Womack v. Munson,* 619 F.2d 1292 (8th Cir. 1980), *cert. denied,* 450 U.S. 979 (1981).

As is evident from the burdens of proof, the most important evidence a supervisor can provide in order to overcome an allegation of discrimination is information regarding the legitimate, nondiscriminatory reason behind a personnel action. This means that at every stage of the process, including the counseling stage, the supervisor should be candid and provide the information which justified the action challenged by the employee. This information is essential to the agency in rebutting an allegation of discrimination and may even result in a withdrawal or settlement of the EEO complaint.

Filing Suit

Under the 1991 Civil Rights Act, employees claiming they have been the victim of discrimination can file suit in U.S. District Court within 90 days of termination of agency or EEOC processing of their complaint. Once in U.S. District Court, a complainant may request a jury trial and seek compensatory (pain and suffering) damages up to $300,000 from the defendant agency.

These two additional features of the EEO system will only be made available to complainants alleging discriminatory acts that took place after November 21, 1991, when the new Civil Rights Act became law. These remedies do not apply to EEO complaints pending at the time the 1991 Civil Rights Act was enacted.

Discrimination And The EEO System

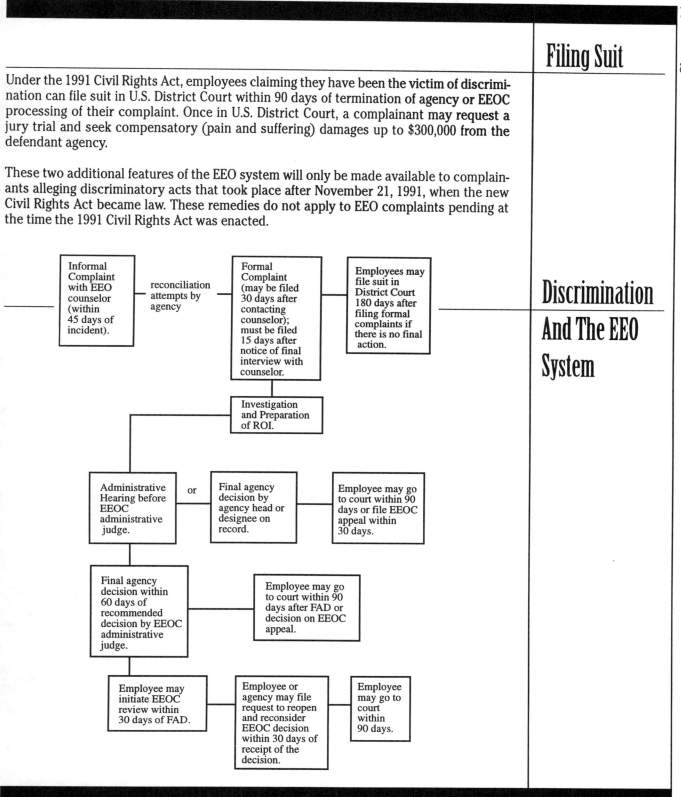

Sexual Harassment

FPMII
COMMUNICATIONS

Sexual Harassment

Determination of whether specific conduct constitutes sexual harassment is made on a case-by-case basis by evaluating all the circumstances.

Sexual harassment is prohibited in the federal workplace and is recognized in the law as a type of sex discrimination proscribed by Title VII of the Civil Rights Act of 1964. Many different types of conduct may constitute sexual harassment, including unwelcome sexual advances, requests for sexual favors, and other verbal or physical conduct of a sexual nature where the person making the advances distinctly states or implies that the other person must submit to the advances as a condition of the person's continued employment, hiring or promotion. Sexual harassment also includes unwelcome advances or comments of a sexual nature that unreasonably interfere with the individual's work performance or create a hostile, intimidating and uncomfortable atmosphere at work. Same-sex sexual harassment/hostile environment claims have been considered by the courts, in cases involving homosexuality; *see Teitgen v. Brown's Westminster Motor Inc.,* No. 1:95cv1095 (U.S.D.C. at Alexandria April 18, 1996).

☑ CASE IN POINT

Susan works at a federal agency. Susan's supervisor, Kevin, routinely makes inappropriate comments about her "sexy" appearance and expresses an interest in dating her. These comments upset and frighten Susan because Kevin is her supervisor. She makes a point of telling Kevin that she is not interested in dating him. She also asks Kevin to stop commenting about her appearance. In spite of her requests, Kevin increases his attentions to Susan and begins sending her love notes, in which he reiterates his interest in her and states that he wishes to have sexual intercourse with her. These comments upset and intimidate Susan to the point where she is reluctant to talk to this supervisor about even work-related matters. She also begins to suffer stomach problems from stress, requiring her to take sick leave and seek medical treatment.

This unwanted attention from Kevin could be construed as creating a hostile and intimidating work environment for Susan because it affects her work; see Howard v. Dep't. of the Air Force, 877 F.2d 952 (Fed. Cir. 1989); Carosella v. U.S. Postal Service, 816 F.2d 638 (Fed. Cir. 1987).

The determination of whether specific conduct constitutes sexual harassment is highly fact-specific. Such a determination is, therefore, made on a case-by-case basis by evaluating all the surrounding circumstances, such as the type of sexual approaches that were made, as well as the context in which the advances were made; *see Meritor Savings Bank v. Vinson,* 477 U.S. 57 (1986). (29 U.S.C. 1604.11) In cases alleging hostile environment sexual harassment, evidence of actual psychological harm is not required to prove sexual harassment. However, an employee making such a claim will be required to show both, that a so called "reasonable person" would think that the work environment was hostile and abusive, and that the employee thought the environment was hostile and abusive. Whether a particular environment is hostile and abusive would depend on factors such as frequency of the discriminatory conduct; severity of the conduct; whether the conduct is threatening or humiliating; whether the conduct consists of merely an offensive utterance; and whether the conduct unreasonably interferes with an employee's work performance; *see Harris v. Forklift Systems, Inc.,* 114 S.Ct. 367 (1993). Notably, the Merit Systems Protection Board (MSPB) has found that conduct that may not constitute sexual harassment under the standards set by Title VII may nevertheless constitute misconduct sufficient to support a disciplinary action, if the conduct at issue violates accepted rules of conduct expected of a supervisor, or violates agency policies or rules regarding sexual harassment; *see, e.g., Jordan v. U.S. Postal Service,* 44 M.S.P.R. 225 (1990); *Anderson v. Dep't. of the Air Force,* 42 M.S.P.R. 644 (1989).

☑ CASE IN POINT

Wade, a postal supervisor, occasionally makes unwarranted sexually explicit comments to female subordinates. He also makes suggestive remarks to several other female employees he does not supervise and, on one occasion, touched one of these employees on her face. The agency may take disciplinary action against this supervisor for violating the standards of conduct expected of a supervisor. If the agency does not charge him with violating anti-discrimination laws aimed at sexual harassment, then the agency will only have to demonstrate that the supervisor's actions violated agency standards of conduct and will not be required to prove that this conduct violated Title VII. However, the fact that this supervisor touched a female employee could be considered a particularly egregious action, which warrants an enhancement of the penalty imposed by the agency; see Pugh v. U.S. Postal Service, 20 M.S.P.R. 326 (1984).

Sexual harassment also occurs in situations where job advancement or benefits are granted to one employee, who submits to the employer's sexual advances or requests for sexual favors, at the expense of another employee who is qualified for, but denied, the same job opportunity or benefit.

☑ CASE IN POINT

Mary and Donna are employed at the Department of Education. Mary has been employed by the agency for five years and has received an "outstanding" rating on her performance appraisal each year. Donna has been employed in an identical position for two years. Both years, Donna has received only a "fully successful" rating on her performance appraisal. Joe, their supervisor, is considering both Mary and Donna for a promotion. Mary is better qualified for the job than Donna. Donna receives the promotion, so Mary files an EEO complaint against the agency, alleging that Donna received the promotion because Donna has been granting Joe's requests for sexual favors. Joe had made similar requests of Mary, but Mary had rejected his advances. If Mary's allegations are true, the agency could be held liable for illegally discriminating against Mary; 29 C.F.R. 1604.11(g); cf. Special Counsel v. Russell, 32 M.S.P.R. 115 (1987).

Agency Responsibility To Prevent Sexual Harassment

The agency is ultimately responsible for sexual harassment that occurs at work, unless it takes immediate action as soon as it becomes aware of the harassment.

An agency is responsible for the actions of its employees, supervisors and managers with respect to any sexual harassment that occurs at the workplace or elsewhere when the employee is acting within the scope of his employment. This means that the agency is ultimately responsible for the acts of supervisors who harass subordinate employees, even if the agency expressly forbids sexual harassment or is not apprised of the harassment in a particular instance. With respect to conduct between fellow employees, the agency is responsible for sexual harassment that occurs at work, unless the agency takes immediate and appropriate corrective action as soon as it becomes aware of the harassment. The MSPB and the Court of Appeals for the Federal Circuit have approved of disciplinary measures taken against employees who sexually harass other employees in the workplace; *see, e.g., Carosella v. U.S. Postal Service,* 30 M.S.P.R. 199 (1986), *aff'd,* 816 F.2d 638 (Fed. Cir. 1987); *see also Ellison v. Brady,* 924 F. 2d 872 (9th Cir. 1991) (requiring employees to take disciplinary action sufficient to ensure a workplace free from sexual harassment).

☑ CASE IN POINT

Bill is a supervisor at the Department of Energy. On several occasions Bill has counseled Ed, one of the employees who works under his supervision, that he should not make sexual advances toward his female co-workers.

Several female employees have complained to Bill that Ed makes suggestive comments to them and touches them without their permission. Ed knows that his actions are improper. In spite of his knowledge about Ed's activities, Bill assigns Ed to work on a project which requires Ed to travel overnight with a female co-worker named Marilyn. Ed is Marilyn's supervisor. When Marilyn returns to the office the day after the overnight trip with Ed, she complains to Bill that Ed repeatedly made sexual advances toward her and tried to force his way into her motel room. If Marilyn files an EEO complaint against the agency in general and against Ed in particular, she could win, absent other circumstances, because the agency is responsible for sexual harassment by its supervisors against other employees. This is true even in this situation, where Bill told Ed to stop his harassing activities. If Ed had been Marilyn's co-worker rather than her supervisor, the agency could still be held responsible for Ed's conduct, unless the agency can show that immediate and appropriate corrective action was taken as soon as Marilyn brought the matter to Bill's attention. Such action might include disciplining Ed or transferring him to another worksite, away from Marilyn; 29 C.F.R. 1604.11(d); *cf. Meritor Savings Bank v. Vinson,* 477 U.S. 57, 74 (1986) (Marshall, J., concurring).

The agency may also be held responsible for the acts of non-employees who sexually harass the agency's employees at the workplace, if the agency knows or should have known that the harassment was occurring and did not take immediate and appropriate corrective action. In eviewing these cases, the Equal Employment Opportunity Commission (EEOC) will consider the extent of control the agency has over the wrongdoer.

☑ CASE IN POINT

Molly is an employee at the Pentagon. The Pentagon has hired contractors to remove asbestos from the corridors of the Pentagon. One of the contractors' employees repeatedly harasses Molly every morning as she enters the office by telling off-color jokes and making other sexually suggestive comments. Molly brings the matter to the attention of her supervisor, Mike. Mike tells Molly that he is sorry the contractor's employee makes her feel uncomfortable, but that since the contractor's employee does not work for the Department of Defense, the agency cannot control his behavior. Mike is mistaken. The agency should contact the contractor immediately and demand that its employee stop harassing the agency's employees. If the contractor's employee continues to bother Molly, the agency should take steps to hire a new contractor. If the agency does not do this, the agency could be held responsible for the contractor's behavior; 29 C.F.R. 1604.11(e); cf. Garziano v. E. I. DuPont & Co., 818 F.2d 380, 387 (5th Cir. 1987).

Prevention is the agency's most effective tool in eliminating sexual harassment at the workplace.

Checklist For Eliminating Sexual Harassment
✓   Frequently and directly discuss the issue.
✓   Express strong disapproval.
✓   Discipline those who sexually harass other employees.
✓   Regularly advise of the right to file sexual harassment complaints.
✓   Be discreet and sensitive when processing complaints.

Prevention is the agency's most effective tool in eliminating sexual harassment at the workplace. The agency should, therefore, take reasonable steps to ensure that all of its employees work in a harassment-free environment.

The following measures are suggested as a means of educating agency employees and of encouraging the elimination of sexual harassment in the workplace:

- The agency should frequently and directly discuss the issue with all of its supervisors and employees to make certain that every worker understands what sexual harassment is, and that it is prohibited.

- The agency (and every supervisor and management official in the agency) should express strong disapproval for even the slightest signs of sexual harassment.

- The agency should institute reprimands and other appropriate penalties for individuals who sexually harass employees and should regularly communicate to its employees the nature of those reprimands and penalties.

- The agency should regularly inform employees of their right to raise sexual harassment complaints and should provide advice to employees about how allegations should be reported and how complaints will be processed.

- The agency should develop methods for processing sexual harassment complaints in a discreet and sensitive manner. Careful attention should be paid to the issue of sexual harassment, including sensitivity to the rights and needs of the victim, and firm, effective discipline for offenders. Methods of filing complaints should include at least two separate individuals to whom the employee can report.

Handicap Discrimination, Disability and Fitness For Duty

Handicap Discrimination, Disability & Fitness For Duty

Handicap

Congress enacted handicap discrimination laws for the federal workforce with the intent that the federal government serve as a progressive, model employer of the handicapped. Congress expected, for example, that if the federal government demonstrated that many physically and mentally handicapped individuals make valuable contributions in the federal workforce, private industry would follow its example by increasing its efforts to permit handicapped employees to make equally valuable contributions in the private sector. Thus, under present law, the federal government has an affirmative obligation to seek out, hire, and accommodate handicapped employees. (29 C.F.R. 1614.703(b) and (c); 29 U.S.C. 791)

Employee Defined

In the federal workplace, a handicapped employee is one who has, or is regarded as having, a mental or physical impairment which significantly limits one or more of the worker's major life activities, such as walking, seeing, hearing, speaking, breathing, learning, working or caring for himself. (29 C.F.R. 1614.203(a)) Diseases, such as tuberculosis, back conditions and learning disabilities, are generally recognized as handicaps. Conditions, such as fear of heights, left-handedness and varicose veins, are not considered to be handicaps, because they do not interfere with major life functions. Temporary conditions, such as a broken leg, are not handicaps within the meaning of the regulations. Additionally, at least one federal court has held that an employee who receives daily radiation treatment for breast cancer is not disabled under federal handicap laws.

Reasonable Accommodation And The Qualified Handicapped Employee

The law states that each federal agency has an obligation to make "reasonable accommodation" to each "qualified handicapped employee" unless the agency can demonstrate that the accommodation would impose an undue hardship on the operation of its program. (29 C.F.R. 1614.203(c)) This means that the agency must work with its handicapped employees to make the physical facilities accessible to handicapped persons. In addition, the agency must restructure the employee's job, including making adjustments to schedules, equipment and examinations to the extent these "accommodations," or adjustments, do not impose an undue hardship on the agency's overall day-to-day activities.

The agency is only required to make these reasonable accommodations to "qualified" handicapped employees, i.e., to those workers who, with or without the accommodation, can perform the essential functions of the job without endangering the health and safety of the handicapped individual or others. The qualified handicapped employee must meet the experience and/or educational requirements for the position or meet the criteria for appointment under one of the special appointing authorities for handicapped persons. (29 C.F.R. 1614.203(a))

The Equal Employment Opportunity Commission (EEOC) regulations define a reasonable accommodation as "any change in the work environment or in the way things are customarily done that enables an individual with a disability to enjoy equal opportunities." 29 C.F.R. 1630.2(o)) Reasonable accommodation could include "job restructuring, part-time or modified work schedules, reassignment to a vacant position, acquisition or modification of equipment or devices, appropriate adjustment or modifications of examinations, training materials or policies [and] the provision of qualified readers or interpreters." 42 U.S.C. 1211(9)(B)) An employee should be expected to participate in the accommodations process by assisting the employer in determining what accommodation is needed.

☑ CASE IN POINT

An employee at the Department of Treasury claimed handicap discrimination based on the agency's failure to promote him from the GS-12 to the GS-13 level. The Merit Systems Protection Board (MSPB) found the employee's appeal to be unpersuasive based upon the employee's failure to demonstrate that he was a qualified handicapped employee. The employee presented medical evidence that he was mentally qualified for the position at the GS-12 level, yet provided no information that he could perform the duties of the GS-13 position or any other GS-13 position.

To establish a prima facie case of handicap discrimination, the employee must demonstrate that he could perform the essential duties of the GS-13 position with or without reasonable accommodation. The employee's appeal based on handicap discrimination was dismissed; see Gavette v. Dep't. of Treasury, 44 M.S.P.R. 166 (1990).

☑ CASE IN POINT

An employee was determined to be a "qualified handicapped employee" based on his demonstration that he could perform the duties of the position in question, which had been restructured to remove non-essential duties such as lifting heavy objects, which he could not perform. With this accommodation, the employee could perform the essential duties of his position and was entitled to the accommodation of assignment to that position; see Green v. U.S. Postal Service, 47 M.S.P.R. 661 (1991).

> The agency is not required to make reasonable accommodation where the accommocation would impose "undue hardship" on the agency.

The agency is not required to make reasonable accommodations in cases where the accommodations would impose an "undue hardship" on the agency. In determining whether an accommodation would impose an undue hardship on the agency, several factors are considered, such as the overall size of the agency's program, the number of its employees, the number and type of its facilities and the size of its budget. Other factors that are considered are the type of agency operation, including the structure of the agency's work force, and the extent of the cost the agency would incur in making the accommodation. When it is impossible or impractical to accommodate the employee, or when an employee is unable to perform the essential functions of his position, even with reasonable accommodation, the agency must offer to reassign the employee to a job he can perform successfully, even with his handicap, when such reassignment would not cause an undue hardship in the operation of the agency's program. (29 C.F.R. 1614.203(g))

While the law is still developing on what constitutes reasonable accommodation and to what extent it is considered "reasonable," at least one court has stated that an employer is not necessarily required to find another job within the agency for an employee who is no longer qualified for his or her current job. This appears to conflict somewhat with the EEOC's regulation or reassignment.

A qualified handicapped employee or applicant for employment has the burden of identifying a reasonable accommodation which will enable him to do the job and demonstrating its feasibility.

☑ CASE IN POINT

In one case, the MSPB upheld the Department of the Air Force's removal of a qualified handicapped employee because of his physical inability to perform the duties of his position. The employee had a qualified handicapping condition of a lower-back disability. The employee was physically unable to perform his part-time Food Service Worker duties at the time of his removal. The agency was unable to restructure his job to enable him to perform his duties, and there were no vacant part-time positions for which he was qualified and to which he could be reassigned. The MSPB upheld the employee's removal, finding that the requirement that an agency accommodate a handicapped employee is not infinite. While the agency must search its vacancies and take other potentially fruitful steps, it need not consider reassignment indefinitely or create a position where none exists; see Patrick v. Dep't. of Air Force, 39 M.S.P.R. 392 (1988).

A qualified handicapped employee or applicant for employment has the burden of identifying a reasonable accommodation which will enable him to do the job, and demonstrating that the accommodation is feasible. The employee or applicant challenging an employment decision must come forward with plausible reasons to believe that his or her handicap could have been accommodated without modifying the essential nature of the position or imposing an undue burden on the employer.

The employer must then come forward with reasons why the accommodation presented by the employee is not feasible. Thus, in making an employment decision involving a handicapped employee, it is important to document the agency's considerations regarding accommodations, and demonstrate that they are plausible, or show why the accommodations may not work or may impose an undue burden on the employer's operations.

☑ CASE IN POINT

Doug is an auditor for the General Services Administration. He is paralyzed from the waist down and confined to a wheelchair.

Doug is randomly assigned to conduct a three-month audit at another federal agency. The building in which Doug must work has no wheelchair access ramp. The only available access to the building is by walking. Doug is perfectly capable of conducting the audit, but he cannot get to the job site due to the wheelchair barrier. Unless it will create an undue hardship, the agency must reasonably accommodate Doug to help him get to the job site. The agency may do this, for example, by installing a ramp, having the audit materials moved to another building, or assigning Doug another case in a building which has a wheelchair access ramp; 29 C.F.R. 1614.203(f); cf. Stanley v. Dep't. of Justice, 48 M.S.P.R. 1 (1991).

☑ CASE IN POINT

Mary is a blind tax auditor at the Department of the Treasury who answers telephone inquiries concerning tax returns. Mary has requested that the agency obtain a copy of the IRS Code in braille to assist her in analyzing cases and responding to inquiries.

Since this accommodation would not create an undue hardship on the agency, this accommodation to assist her should be provided; but see Carter v. Bennett, 840 F.2d 63 (D.C. Cir. 1988) *(where a visually impaired employee's request for accommodation which included a voice-synthesized computer and two floppy disc drives was held to be unnecessary for adequate performance and therefore unreasonable);* cf. Miller v. Dep't. of Navy, 42 M.S.P.R. 10 (1989).

☑ CASE IN POINT

Cliff is a letter carrier with the Postal Service. After he is permanently injured in an accident, Cliff is no longer able to walk. Since mobility is an essential function of his job as a letter carrier, the agency may remove him from his position without making a reasonable accommodation. The agency is not required to eliminate one of the essential functions of a job, i.e., delivering mail, as an accommodation. The agency must, however, try to find another position for Cliff within the Postal Service where his loss of mobility would not prevent him from performing the job; see Ignacio v. U.S. Postal Service, 16 M.S.P.R. 530 (1983); Ignacio v. U.S. Postal Service, 30 M.S.P.R. 471 (Spec. Pan. 1986); 29 C.F.R. 1614.203(g).

☑ CASE IN POINT

Susan works at the Library of Congress. As the result of an injury, she suffers from a reading disability that interferes with her ability to catalog materials, which is required by her job duties. Since she often reads the titles incorrectly, many of the materials are improperly filed. The agency is not required to restructure the performance standards of Susan's job to accommodate her handicap. Employees who have reading or learning disabilities, or those who are mentally retarded, can be held to the same standards as other employees who perform the same job. If the agency cannot reassign Susan to a job she can perform, she can be removed from the agency for her inability to perform the essential functions of the job; see Jasany v. U.S. Postal Service, 755 F.2d 1244 (6th Cir. 1985).

Fitness For Duty

A fitness for duty inquiry can be initiated in response to employee-provided medical evidence and under other very limited circumstances. (5 C.F.R. 339.301(a)) For example, an agency may require a physical examination for an individual who has applied for or occupies a position which has medical standards or physical requirements that existed prior to appointment or selection. The examination may occur: 1) on a regular or periodic basis after appointment, or 2) whenever there is a direct question about an employee's continued capacity to meet the physical or medical requirements of a position. (5 C.F.R. 339.301(b))

☑ CASE IN POINT

An employee, a GS-9 Supervisory Social Science Technician, was ordered by his agency to submit to a fitness for duty examination, although the employee's position had no physical or medical requirements. Noting that, because of previous abuses, the fitness for duty examination regulations had been revised to limit significantly the authority of agencies to order medical examinations for employees, particularly in cases involving psychiatric examinations and disability retirement, the MSPB held that evidence obtained through the illegally-ordered fitness for duty examination could not be relied upon in taking an adverse action against the employee; see Collins v. Dep't. of Navy, 41 M.S.P.R. 256 (1989).

An agency may order a psychiatric examination only when: 1) the results of a current general medical examination, which the agency has the authority to order, indicate no physical explanation for behavior which may affect the safe and efficient performance of the individual or others, or 2) a psychiatric examination is specifically called for in a position having medical standards. (5 C.F.R. 339.301(e)) An agency may offer a medical examination, including a psychiatric evaluation, in any situation where the agency needs additional medical documentation to make informed management decisions, such as when an individual requests, for medical reasons, a change in duty status or working conditions, a reassignment, or any special treatment, including reasonable accommodation. (5 C.F.R. 339.302)

The fitness for duty regulations have been in effect since 1984 and are a marked departure from prior practices. The changes were made to correct agency abuses in ordering fitness for duty exams and agency-initiated disability retirements, particularly in the area of psychiatric examination. The current focus is on the employee's job performance or conduct. While an agency should be sensitive to a medical condition, current law indicates that, for most jobs, the employee must raise the issue and provide the evidence.

Disabled Employees

An agency can remove a disabled employee who can no longer provide useful service in his job or in another position at the same grade level in the same geographic area. If the employee is covered under the Civil Service Retirement System (CSRS), and has five or more years of service, the employee will be eligible for disability retirement.

Similarly, if the employee is covered under the Federal Employees' Retirement System (FERS), and has 18 months or more of service, he is eligible to apply for disability retirement. (5 U.S.C. 8337 (CSRS); 5 U.S.C. 8451 (FERS))

The agency has only limited authority to apply for disability retirement on behalf of a disabled employee. (5 C.F.R. 831.1203) As such, the employee, his family member, or his legal representative has the burden of completing and submitting the application for disability retirement.

This must be done within one year of the employee's removal from federal service. In some cases where the agency issues a decision to remove the employee based on reasons which on their face appear to be caused by a medical condition, the agency is required to advise the employee in writing that he may be eligible for disability retirement. (5 C.F.R. 831.1203(b))

The Alcohol Or Drug Dependent Employee

The Alcohol Or Drug Dependent Employee

Chapter 16 discusses the steps that a federal agency may take to accommodate, or assist, its "qualified handicapped employees" in performing their work. Employees with alcohol or drug dependencies can be considered to be a "qualified handicapped individual" under the law. Prior to 1992, an agency had the obligation to reasonably accommodate such a handicap. Such accommodations included the requirement that agencies offer the employee counseling and treatment, as well as a "firm choice" agreement before removing the employee. After 1992, however, Congress amended the Rehabilitation Act to conform with Title I of the Americans with Disabilities Act. In effect, this amendment provides that an agency may hold an alcoholic or drug dependent employee to the same performance/conduct standards as other employees, even if the employee's poor performance or misconduct is due to the alcoholism. Thus, while an agency should grant an employee reasonable accommodation, such as a flexible schedule or leave to seek treatment, the agency is no longer required to offer an employee a "firm choice" agreement.

☑ CASE IN POINT

Harry has an ongoing battle with alcohol. Because of his alcoholism, he has a pattern of misconduct, including sleeping on duty and tardiness. The agency does not know for certain that Harry is an alcoholic, but it presumes that he has such a problem due to its observation of Harry's conduct and behavior. The agency has used progressive discipline to control Harry's attendance problems, including suspending him. The agency has also proposed his removal, but reduced it to a suspension, with a warning that he should seek counseling if he has an alcohol problem. Harry placed himself into a short-term treatment program and the agency granted him leave to attend. The agency later learned, however, that Harry did not complete the program. The agency then proposed his removal for AWOL and for providing false information to the agency regarding his attendance in the treatment program. Although the agency never entered into an official "firm choice" agreement with Harry, it may fire him; see Kimble v. Dep't of Navy, 70 M.S.P.R. 617 (1996).

Agency's Ability To Assist Employees With Substance Abuse Problems

Although an agency is no longer required to offer an employee a "firm choice," it may still be required to offer other reasonable accommodations. However, it is important to note that the agency is not precluded from offering a "firm choice" agreement.

Once an agency detects that one of its employees may have a substance dependence problem, the agency should tell the employee about counseling services that are available. One such service is the employee assistance program (EAP). If the employee's performance remains unsatisfactory due to the substance abuse problem, the agency may remove the employee or may offer the employee a "firm choice" between treatment of the problem and disciplinary action.

In a "firm choice" agreement, the agency gives the employee an unequivocal choice between effective treatment of his condition and initiation of removal procedures. The firm choice should specify that removal will be proposed if any one or more of five (5) enumerated circumstances occurs. A threat that the employee "could be subject to discipline" does not constitute a firm choice; *see Yancy v. General Services Administration,* 57 M.S.P.R. 192 (1993).

The enumerated circumstances that will result in proposed removal are if the employee: 1) chooses not to participate in a treatment program; 2) ceases such participation; 3) is discharged from such a program prior to completion; 4) fails to adhere to the terms of the program; or 5) engages in future alcohol-related misconduct or has future alcohol-related performance deficiencies; *see Harris v. Dep't. of Army,* 57 M.S.P.R. 124 (1993).

The underlying policy goal of a properly worded "firm choice" is to provide finality, predictability and specificity to the employee by placing the employee on clear notice of the problem, the recommended solution and the consequences. The agency is saying that it will no longer tolerate the problem and is prepared to undertake final resolution. Discipline short of removal is an acceptable accommodation for alcoholism only where a "firm choice" is offered at the time the discipline is imposed and an opportunity for rehabilitation is also offered by the agency at that time; *see Banks v. Dep't. of Navy,* 57 M.S.P.R. 141 (1993).

As stated above, the agency is not required to offer a "firm choice" agreement. However, it is advisable, in the interest of good employee relations, for the agency to use its best efforts to assist the employee in overcoming his problem. Nevertheless, there may be several reasons why an agency may not want to offer an employee a "firm choice."

For example, there may be circumstances when an employee's alcohol-related misconduct is so egregious, that the agency is not required to provide any reasonable accommodation prior to terminating the employee. In such circumstances, the employee's conduct will be found to have placed him outside of the protections of the Rehabilitation Act because he is no longer a "qualified handicapped employee;" *see Alex v. U.S. Postal Service,* 38 M.S.P.R. 605 (1988). In addition, an agency may not accommodate an employee with a substance abuse problem if the employee engages in misconduct which, by its very nature, strikes at the core of the agency's mission, or is so egregious or notorious that the employee's ability to perform his duties or to represent his agency is hampered; *see Hougens v. U.S. Postal Service,* 38 M.S.P.R. 135 (1988).

Unless it is clear that the employee's problem warrants in-patient treatment, he should be permitted to participate in an out-patient treatment program long enough to reasonably cure the substance abuse problem. For example, an employee who has abused alcohol may, through participation in Alcoholics Anonymous meetings each evening, permanently refrain from alcohol abuse. If the employee discontinues the out-patient treatment before he successfully completes the program, or if the employee engages in job-related misconduct caused by the substance dependence, generally the agency should permit the employee to participate in an in-patient program before terminating him. However, an employee is not considered a qualified handicapped employee if his substance abuse prob-

---

> In a "firm choice" agreement, the agency gives the employee an unequivocal choice between effective treatment for his condition and initiation of removal procedures.

Out-Patient And In-Patient Treatment— The Firm Choice

> Once an agency permits an employee to begin rehabilitation, the employee must be given reasonable opportunity to complete the program.

lem prevents him from performing the essential functions of his position or if his presence causes a direct threat to the employer's property or to the safety of other employees; *see Malbouf v. Dep't. of the Army*, 43 M.S.P.R. 588 (1990); *Hougens v. U.S. Postal Service*, 38 M.S.P.R. 135 (1988). The agency also may authorize the employee to use accrued or unpaid leave to attend in-patient treatment. Once an agency permits an employee to begin a rehabilitation program, the employee must be given a reasonable opportunity to complete the program; *see Calton v. Dep't. of the Army*, 44 M.S.P.R. 477 (1990; *Hodge v. Dep't. of the Air Force*, 39 M.S.P.R. 174 (1988).

☑ CASE IN POINT

Gordon has serious attendance problems, which his supervisor thinks are alcohol-related. After talking with his agency's Employee Assistance Program counselor, Gordon begins to attend Alcoholics Anonymous meetings on October 1st. The agency should not terminate him if he has not stopped his alcohol abuse by October 8th. It is not reasonable to expect that Gordon would completely refrain from drinking after one week.

However, if Gordon has not shown any improvement after several months and his attendance problems continue or worsen, the agency might be justified in disciplining him for repeated instances of alcohol-related absenteeism, as several months may be a reasonable opportunity to show improvement. However, if the agency decides to terminate Gordon, he should first be offered the opportunity to attend in-patient treatment. If Gordon refuses to attend or the treatment is unsuccessful, he may then be terminated; cf. Simms v. U.S. Postal Service, 39 M.S.P.R. 308 (1989).

In contrast, the agency may decide to terminate an employee before he receives any treatment if the employee's attendance in an in-patient treatment center would cause the agency undue hardship. Thus, using the above example, if Gordon's addiction is so severe that his rehabilitation may require a treatment of three to four months, the agency may find it necessary to replace Gordon immediately. In addition, the agency may decide to remove an employee who completes in-patient treatment but then relapses, if the relapse results in the employee's renewed inability to perform his work satisfactorily. In this situation, however, the agency should consider the length of time that the employee has abstained from substance abuse. If the employee has abstained for a long period of time before the relapse, such as a year, and the employee's performance was improved during the period of abstinence, the agency might decide to give the employee another chance at rehabilitation; *see Rodgers v. Lehman*, 869 F.2d 253 (4th Cir. 1989). While an agency is not generally required to provide repeated opportunities for rehabilitation after one failed attempt, if the agency does so, the employee should be permitted to complete the subsequent rehabilitation programs and demonstrate improvement at work prior to the agency taking serious disciplinary action.

Employee Challenges To Adverse Actions

The employee

will have to

demonstrate that

the conduct

causing the

agency's disciplin-

ary action was a

manifestation of

the substance

abuse problem.

In instances where the agency proposes an adverse action against the employee and the employee wishes to raise substance dependence as a defense, the employee must demonstrate that he is handicapped by substance abuse and that there is a link between his substance abuse and the conduct that allegedly supports the agency's adverse action.

In order to demonstrate that he is handicapped by substance abuse, the employee must show that the abuse is extensive and that it actually affects him. This means that the employee may be required to show actual addiction, as opposed to casual or weekend use. The employee may also be required to provide testimony from witnesses with personal knowledge of the extent of the substance abuse, as well as medical evidence. In this regard, the employee's burden of proof is similar to any other handicap discrimination case. The employee will also have to demonstrate that the conduct causing the agency's disciplinary action was a manifestation of the substance abuse problem.

☑ CASE IN POINT

Ralph, an alcoholic, works at a federal agency as a computer specialist. At lunch he frequently drinks and occasionally returns to work intoxicated. Initially, his agency is unaware of his alcohol problem. But later, it becomes obvious because over time Ralph's lunchtime drinking increases to the point where he does not return to work from lunch for several hours and sometimes does not return at all. After repeated warnings, the agency begins to charge Ralph as absent without leave (AWOL) when he is late or does not return from lunch. After several incidents of AWOL, the agency proposes to suspend Ralph for 30 days because of his unauthorized absences.

At the Merit Systems Protection Board (MSPB), Ralph could prevail if he presents: 1) evidence and testimony that his absences from work were caused by his substance dependence and alcohol-impaired judgment, and 2) testimony from his physician that he has an alcohol-dependence problem. Once this evidence is presented, the agency may be required to permit Ralph to take leave in order to get assistance for his problem; cf. Terry v. Dep't. of Navy, 39 M.S.P.R. 565 (1989). If Ralph cannot prove that he is otherwise able to meet job performance standards, however, he may not prevail because an agency is not required to excuse the violation of uniformly-applied job conduct or job performance standards as a form of reasonable accommodation; see Kimble v. Dep't of Navy, 70 M.S.P.R. 617 (1996).

In cases where the agency proposes to remove an employee for unsatisfactory job performance caused by the employee's substance abuse, the employee may be treated as a qualified handicapped employee if he can show that there is a link between his substance abuse and the adverse action proposed by the agency. In some instances, however, the employee MAY NOT raise his substance abuse as a defense.

In some instances, an employee MAY NOT use his substance abuse as a defense.

This means that the agency may remove the employee notwithstanding the fact that his poor performance or misconduct is caused by his substance abuse in the following types of cases:

- Removal due to the employee's egregious or criminal activity—relating to drugs or alcohol;

- Removal due to the employee's absenteeism and falsification of leave forms;

- Removal due to the employee's misappropriation of agency funds;

- Removal due to the employee's irregular work schedule;

- Removal due to the employee's misconduct when the agency is unaware of the employee's substance abuse problem;

- Removal due to the employee's poor performance when performance did not improve during periods of abstinence;

- Removal due to the employee's failure to provide adequate documentation to support his request for sick leave;

- Removal due to the employee's denial of a security clearance due to a substance abuse problem;

- Removal due to off-duty conduct which disqualifies the employee from his particular position (e.g., law enforcement position), or which causes the employee to lose qualifications required for performance of his job, such as a driver's license; and

- Removal due to off-duty conduct which demonstrates that the person's employment may pose a threat to the safety of others.

☑ CASE IN POINT

James, an alcoholic, was employed at a hospital for several years. James' problem with alcohol escalated to the point that he would black out for a period of time when he was drinking. While on leave from the hospital, and while he was in a black-out, James went to the hospital and got in a violent scuffle with security guards. Although James did not remember the event because he was intoxicated, he was removed from employment. The hospital was justified in terminating James, as it determined that he was a threat to the hospital and its employees; see Johnson v. New York Hospital, 5 A.D. 1537 (September 13, 1996) (2nd Cir.).

☑ CASE IN POINT

Don is employed at a federal agency. Although he is an alcoholic, he has not had any serious problems at work. However, one day after work, Don went on a drinking rampage that ended up in a bar where Don pulled out an assault rifle and threatened to fire it at individuals in the bar. Don was arrested and later fired from his job. The agency was justified in firing Don because his off-duty actions constituted "notoriously disgraceful conduct" that was above and beyond any disability he may suffer; see Newland v. Dalton, 81 F.3d 904 (9th Cir. 1996).

Types of Employee Conduct or Performance Not Requiring Accommodation Because of Alcohol or Drug Abuse
◆   Drug-related criminal activity.
◆   Falsification of leave form.
◆   Misappropriation of agency funds.
◆   Irregular work schedule.
◆   Misconduct when the agency is unaware of substance abuse.
◆   Poor performance that does not improve during abstinence.
◆   Inadequate documentation for sick leave.
◆   Denial of security clearance.
◆   Loss of a job qualification, e.g., a driver's license when such is required for the position.

Changes In The Law

The law in this area is subject to frequent changes. Although the principles discussed in this chapter should serve as helpful guidance, a prudent supervisor should always contact appropriate agency officials to determine the current status of the law whenever he suspects that one of his employees has an alcohol or drug dependence problem.

In September 1990, the Equal Employment Opportunity Commission (EEOC) published a Monograph, entitled *Alcoholism and Drug Abuse as Handicapping Conditions: An Update,* as a part of its monthly publication of *The Digest of EEO Law.* Anyone desiring more information about handling alcoholic or drug dependent employees should contact the EEOC, Office of Federal Operations, 1801 L Street, N.W., Washington, D.C. 20507, (202) 663-4599, for a copy of this comprehensive publication.

Disability Retirement

Remember that employees dependent on drugs and alcohol are disabled and may be eligible for disability retirement if they have 18 months under FERS or five years under the CSRS retirement programs. (5 U.S.C. 8337 (CSRS) and 5 U.S.C. 8451 (FERS) and related OPM regulations at 5 C.F.R. Part 831)

Employees dependent on drugs and alcohol are disabled and may be eligible for disability retirement.

Handling The Problem Employee At The United States Postal Service

Handling The Problem Employee At The United States Postal Service

The United States Postal Service is an independent establishment within the Executive Branch. It was created in 1971 with the enactment of the Postal Reorganization Act (PRA), Title 39, U.S.C. The enactment of the PRA changed the status of the Postal Service and made it different in some ways from other federal agencies in the government.

For example, the PRA created a non-managerial workforce governed by negotiated collective bargaining agreements, in addition to retaining some aspects of federal personnel law. Unlike other federal employee unions, the postal unions are regulated by the National Labor Relations Board (NLRB), instead of the Federal Labor Relations Authority (FLRA). Like other federal employees, however, postal workers are forbidden by law to strike. In addition, the PRA also changed the effects of certain federal personnel laws on postal employees.

This chapter explains significant differences, as well as underscores similarities, in the application of the personnel principles and procedures explained in this book as they apply to Postal Service employees. The primary difference between the Postal Service and other federal agencies is that some laws that are applicable generally to federal employees are not applicable to postal employees, or such laws are applied in a manner that affects appeal rights enjoyed by postal employees.

The Postal Service Workforce

A key to understanding the impact of federal personnel laws on postal employees is an understanding of how the postal workforce is organized. The Postal Service is divided into two categories of employees: bargaining unit or "craft" employees and non-bargaining or "management" employees.

The rights and benefits of bargaining unit or craft employees are determined through collective bargaining between the unions and the Postal Service. Each union has its own collective bargaining agreement with the Postal Service, which provides for such things as leave and insurance benefits, salary rates, seniority and promotions. (39 U.S.C. 1202 through 1206) The collective bargaining agreements also contain grievance-arbitration procedures for resolving employment disputes and interpretations of articles in agreements themselves.

Non-bargaining unit employees perform the managerial functions of the Postal Service. Under the PRA, the rights and benefits of these employees are determined by the Postal Service, although the Act does permit management organizations to meet and confer on an advisory basis with the Postal Service on employee issues. Other employment matters, such as leave accrual, retirement, and performance evaluations are regulated by or with reference to federal law and postal and federal regulations.

Effects of Federal Personnel Laws On Postal Employees

As a general proposition, postal employees are exempt from coverage of federal personnel laws, unless those are specifically made applicable to the United States Postal Service under the PRA (39 U.S.C. 410 and 1005), or by a particular statute. However, many of the same rights and remedies available to other federal sector employees are available to postal employees.

For example, postal employees (both management and craft) are covered by Title VII, Equal Employment Opportunity (EEO) laws and other anti-discrimination laws. Accordingly, postal employees may file complaints of employment discrimination, which are processed through the same regulatory system and procedures as are used by other federal agencies.

Thus, postal managers are prohibited from considering factors such as an individual's sex, race, age, religion, color or national origin when making a personnel decision. With respect to handicapping conditions, including substance abuse problems, postal managers have the same obligations as other federal managers to consider whether reasonable accommodation is possible when making personnel decisions. These principles are discussed in detail in Chapters 16 and 17.

Some postal employees also have the right to appeal adverse actions to the Merit Systems Protection Board (MSPB), as do other federal employees, with some differences unique to the Postal Service. (39 U.S.C. 1005 and 5 U.S.C. 7511) Appealable adverse actions include a suspension of more than 14 days (including instances of enforced leave for more than 14 days), a demotion, and termination of employment. Postal managers and supervisors at level EAS-18 and higher, and preference eligible employees (i.e., veterans, both bargaining and non-bargaining unit) may file appeals of adverse actions with the MSPB. Other non-bargaining unit employees who are not supervisors may also have MSPB appeal rights if they demonstrate that they are engaged in personnel work in other than a purely non-confidential capacity; *see Anmuth v. U.S. Postal Service,* 45 M.S.P.R. 656 (1990); *Benifield v. U.S. Postal Service,* 40 M.S.P.R. 50 (1989). For bargaining unit employees, however, these appeal rights are limited by the collective bargaining agreements negotiated between the postal unions and the Postal Service. Thus, the collective bargaining agreements may require that an employee forego access to arbitration under the applicable collective bargaining agreement if he chooses to appeal an adverse action to the MSPB. Nevertheless, a postal employee may obtain a limited review of an arbitration decision by the MSPB.

☑ CASE IN POINT

Elija, a window clerk with preference eligible rights, was terminated from his position. His removal was stayed, pending his use of the grievance process. He grieved his removal through the procedures in his union's collective bargaining agreement. His union took the grievance to arbitration, and a decision was issued finding that his removal was for just cause. Within 20 days of the effective date of the arbitration award, Elija can appeal his removal to the MSPB. The MSPB will most likely defer to the arbitrator's award, however, unless Elija alleges and proves that the arbitrator erred in interpreting or applying civil service law, rule or regulation; see Williams v. U.S. Postal Service, 35 M.S.P.R. 581 (1987).

Non-preference eligible employees (those without veteran status) in the bargaining unit have no right of appeal to the MSPB. Non-bargaining unit employees below EAS-18 do not have appeal rights to the MSPB; *see Banks v. U.S. Postal Service,* 31 M.S.P.R. 307 (1986). However, these employees do have access to grievance procedures. Bargaining unit employees, through their unions, may utilize the grievance-arbitration procedures established in their collective bargaining agreements. Non-bargaining unit employees who are unable to appeal to the MSPB may appeal adverse actions through the Postal Service's internal grievance procedures, found at Part 650 of the Postal Service's EL-311 Handbook.

Postal employees having appeal rights to the MSPB may seek judicial review of MSPB decisions at the Federal Circuit, the same as any other federal sector employee. As with most internal agency grievance procedures, there is no right of judicial review of a decision under the Part 650 non-bargaining appeals procedure.

Employees who utilize the grievance-arbitration procedures in their collective bargaining agreements have access to judicial review under limited circumstances. For example, an employee whose union has failed to invoke properly the grievance process or pursue an employee's grievance to arbitration may bring an action against the union and/or the Postal Service under the PRA (39 U.S.C. 1208(b)) for breach of the union's duty of fair representation and/or breach of contract. In actions such as these, the union and the Postal Service may be co-defendants and damages may be apportioned between the two parties. A section 1208(b) claim may be brought in any federal district court.

In limited circumstances, either the Postal Service or a postal union may bring suit in federal district court to vacate an arbitration award. However, because the collective bargaining agreements in effect between the postal unions and the Postal Service contain binding arbitration clauses, courts are extremely hesitant to disturb arbitration decisions and will do so only in limited circumstances; *see W.R. Grace & Co. v. Local Union, 759, International Union of United Rubber Workers,* 461 U.S. 757 (1983).

Significant Laws That Do Not Apply To The Postal Service

There are some federal laws that do not apply to the Postal Service at all. One of the most significant of these is the Whistleblower Protection Act of 1989. Under this statute, federal employees, either through the OSC or individually after seeking redress from OSC, may bring claims for relief from actions taken in retaliation for reporting waste, fraud or mismanagement in government operations, or other violations of law, rule or regulation. Such appeals are filed with the MSPB, through which federal employees may seek correction of any adverse action taken against them for retaliatory reasons, or discipline against the individuals who took or threatened to take the disputed adverse action. The Postal Service is exempt from coverage under this statute.

Another significant difference in the Postal Service is that postal employees are not entitled to use their leave and, therefore, may be disciplined for excessive use of even approved leave; *see American Postal Workers Union v. U.S. Postal Service,* 736 F.2d 317 (6th Cir. 1984). However, postal managers who wish to discipline employees for attendance problems should be careful to document the problem and use progressive measures, such as informal counseling sessions, prior to taking formal actions. In addition, managers who supervise bargaining unit employees should consult any Memoranda of Understanding between the local branches of postal unions and their facility, as these agreements sometimes contain special procedures for handling employees with disciplinary problems.

Finally, although non-bargaining postal employees have performance evaluations that are similar to the systems employed by other federal agencies, postal employees cannot challenge their performance appraisals through the MSPB, unless the performance appraisal has resulted in an otherwise appealable adverse action being taken against the employee.* However, as in the rest of the federal sector, non-bargaining postal employees may appeal their evaluations through the Postal Service's internal grievance procedures. Accordingly, postal managers should be careful to document performance problems and provide employees with notice if there are serious deficiencies. These issues are discussed more fully in Chapter 3.

With some significant differences, Postal Service employees have the same rights as any other federal sector employees. Accordingly, most of the management practices discussed elsewhere in this book are applicable to assist postal managers in handling personnel issues that arise with problem employees and in identifying special obligations that a manager may have, such as in cases involving substance abuse/alcohol dependence problems. While in some circumstances the remedies available to a Postal Service employee against whom a personnel action has been taken may be more limited than those available to other federal employees, the postal manager should nevertheless be conscious of adhering to procedural requirements and of generating and maintaining sufficient documentation to support any action taken. Then, in the event a challenge to that action is raised, the manager will be prepared.

> Postal employees are not allowed to use their leave, and may be disciplined for excessive use of even approved leave.

---

*Bargaining unit employees are not evaluated under a merit system and generally are not regularly evaluated at all once they have completed their 90-day probationary period.

Supervisory And Managerial Liability And Exposure In The Face Of Employee Counter-Claims

Supervisory & Managerial Liability And Exposure In The Face Of Employee Counter-Claims

No book about handling problem federal employees would be complete without some discussion concerning the exposure of the federal supervisor and manager to liability from counter-attacks by subordinate employees. Supervisors and managers frequently ask about their personal liability, and they must understand the limited scope of their exposure before they will feel comfortable taking effective action to rehabilitate or remove a problem employee.

As a general rule, a supervisor who takes action against a problem employee for appropriate and lawful reasons need not fear an employee challenge to the use of supervisory authority. The supervisor who feels self-assured about the absence of motivation based on illegal reprisal, discrimination, or other improper factors should not be sidetracked by employee challenges. Instead, he should proceed with the proper rehabilitative effort or adverse action.

For the most part employee challenges fall far short of the mark and do not result in any adverse consequences to a supervisor. In addition, even the best supervisors and managers sometimes have grievances, Equal Employment Opportunity (EEO) complaints, or lawsuits filed against them. Thus, it is not a mark of poor supervision if an employee challenges supervisory or managerial authority.

Awareness of the potential pitfalls and means by which employee challenges occur, however, can help the supervisor avoid trouble spots. The following sections discuss the most common situations in which employee challenges to supervisory or managerial authority occur.

While there are certainly some risks, a well-documented, properly motivated case against a problem employee will seldom pose any real threat to the supervisor or manager.

Adverse Action

A supervisor who acts with improper reasons and motives in recommending or taking an adverse personnel action may, under some circumstances, commit a prohibited personnel practice, which, in turn, is a specific violation of federal personnel law. Examples of prohibited personnel practices are illegal discrimination, whistleblower reprisal, nepotism, providing improper favoritism or injuring the employment prospects of another.

If evidence shows that a supervisor has committed a prohibited personnel practice, such a finding could form the basis for an adverse action against the supervisor, which could even include removal from federal service. However, in order for an adverse action against the supervisor to occur, higher-level authority in the agency must be convinced that the supervisor acted improperly. The complaining employee, who may be alleging an improper, prohibited motive on the part of the supervisor as a diversionary tactic in an adverse action against the employee, has no direct control over such a decision concerning the supervisor.

Furthermore, the supervisor who is subjected to a severe adverse action (such as removal or demotion because of his improper motivation or improper processing of a personnel action against another employee) has the right of appeal to the MSPB. A supervisor may challenge a less severe adverse action (such as a suspension of 14 days or less or a reprimand) through the agency grievance procedure.

Thus, the supervisor is not without a remedy if he is accused by a subordinate employee. The presence of these rights usually prevents unreasonable action as a result of an employee complaint.

☑ CASE IN POINT

A male supervisor was accused of forcing a female subordinate to have sexual relations with him. On the basis of the subordinate's allegations, the agency charged the supervisor with sexual harassment and removed him from his position. The MSPB reversed, finding doubts concerning the reliability of the subordinate's testimony. Specifically, the Board found three important discrepancies or inconsistencies in the evidence presented by the female subordinate concerning the events surrounding the alleged incident. In view of these inconsistencies and the absence of any physical or medical evidence or eyewitness testimony, the MSPB refused to sustain the charges against the supervisor; see Flores v. Dep't. of Labor, 13 M.S.P.R. 281 (1992).

In only rare cases does an agency decide to discipline a supervisor for acting inappropriately toward subordinate employees. When discipline is imposed, the case usually concerns supervisory misconduct that manifests itself in inappropriate supervisory statements about a person's race, sex or national origin, or a physical assault on a subordinate employee. In some instances adverse actions are taken against supervisors who have blatantly ignored employee rights or who have knowingly abused such rights.

For example, a supervisor who assaults a subordinate will probably be subject to an adverse action; *see Andrus v. IRS,* 14 M.S.P.R. 500 (1983) (reducing demotion to a 30-day suspension for a supervisor who struck a subordinate employee in the face with his hand); *Blackford v. Dep't. of the Navy,* 8 M.S.P.R. 712 (1981) (sustaining removal of a supervisory police captain for striking and injuring a subordinate officer, because of the supervisor's important role in furthering the agency obligation to its employees and constituencies and to create and enforce the principle of non-violence within the police ranks).

Again, careful adherence by a supervisor to the rules applicable to handling employee actions, careful documentation of the facts, and good common sense in addressing employee concerns will likely eliminate any possible adverse action against the supervisor.

Careful adherence by a supervisor to the rules for handling employee actions, careful documentation of facts and common sense will likely eliminate possible adverse actions against the supervisor.

Agency Inspector General Investigation

The Inspector General has the authority to investigate mismanagement or failure of agency officials to follow statutes, rules or regulations.

Most federal agencies have an independent, presidentially-appointed Inspector General, who has the authority to investigate mismanagement or the failure of agency officials to follow statutes, rules or regulations. In some instances, as a result of an employee hotline complaint or other referral to an Inspector General, the supervisor may be the subject of an Inspector General investigation. A disgruntled employee will sometimes make a referral about his supervisor to the Inspector General when the employee is under the supervisor's scrutiny. Sometimes this employee challenge is direct and concerns the way the supervisor is handling a particular action that is occurring against the employee. Other times the challenge is indirect and concerns allegations by the employee that the supervisor has engaged in unrelated misconduct, such as filing false travel vouchers or theft of government property.

Inquiries and contacts by an agency Inspector General should be taken seriously. In those instances where contact by the Inspector General seems to be more than a routine effort to clear up what might be viewed as a crank complaint, the supervisor should consider consulting with legal counsel prior to consenting to participate in an interrogation by Office of Inspector General investigators.

However, the supervisor should not allow an Inspector General investigation in and of itself to interfere with a properly motivated and properly processed personnel action against a subordinate employee.

It is relevant that the employee who has made the referral to the Inspector General is being subjected to a personnel action. This often will provide the Inspector General with a good reason to discontinue the investigation of the supervisor. In this circumstance, care must be taken not to retaliate against the employee for his referral to the Inspector General. Remember, however, that it is not retaliation for a supervisor to follow through with a personnel action that can be shown to have been in the planning or processing stages before the employee first contacted the Inspector General.

Inspector General investigations in most agencies do not determine an agency decision whether to take action against a manager or supervisor as a result of a subordinate employee complaint. Instead, decisions on whether to take administrative action are made by higher-level management. Decisions on whether to proceed with a criminal action will always be made by the Department of Justice. Thus, a supervisor would ultimately deal with his higher-level management officials when responding to issues raised by an Inspector General investigation.

The facts in each case vary, but most Inspector General investigations pursued as a result of a referral by a disgruntled employee do not result in a serious threat to supervisory authority. Of course, a supervisor who has misused his position or who has otherwise committed violations of the law, or who is afraid he may be perceived as having engaged in misconduct, should be careful to seek private legal counsel, especially before making any statements to the Inspector General investigators.

Office Of Special Counsel Prosecution

Charged by Congress with enforcing the merit system, OSC investigates and prosecutes federal employees who have committed prohibited personnel practices.

The Office of Special Counsel (OSC) is charged by Congress with enforcing the merit system. As part of this responsibility, the OSC investigates and prosecutes federal employees who, in the opinion of the Office, have committed prohibited personnel practices. (5 U.S.C. 1211-1216) (See Chapter 6 for a summary of the prohibited personnel practices.) The manager or supervisor who is subjected to an OSC investigation may be removed from federal employment, debarred from future federal employment for a period of five years, fined, suspended, demoted or reprimanded. (5 C.F.R. 1201.126(c))

Over the years the OSC has prosecuted few federal employees, but in some cases, the prosecutions have been significant and the punishment severe.

The OSC has broad authority to investigate a prohibited personnel practice. Federal employees are required to cooperate with the OSC, and any federal employee who does not provide information and documents as requested by the Special Counsel can be subjected to discipline by the OSC merely for not cooperating. (5 C.F.R. 5.4) As for federal employees who are the subject of a Special Counsel investigation, each has the right to an attorney and should consider bringing an attorney to both the initial and subsequent interviews that are a part of the investigation.

Prosecution by the OSC is adjudicated by the MSPB. Such prosecution begins with a complaint filed by OSC. The employee against whom the complaint is filed is entitled to answer the complaint and engage in discovery from the OSC to obtain documents and information in OSC's possession relevant to the employee's case.

In addition, the employee is entitled to a hearing before the MSPB and a recommended decision by one of its administrative judges. (5 C.F.R. 1202.124) Further recourse to the MSPB and the courts is available to an employee who is the subject of an OSC prosecution.

Employees should be wary of dealing with OSC, since the Office has a great deal of prosecutorial discretion concerning which cases to pursue. Even if a supervisor's agency believes the supervisor acted appropriately, the employee could be removed from federal employment as a result of an OSC prosecution.

A bit of information about whistleblower reprisal is helpful. The Whistleblower Protection Act (WPA) applies to OSC prosecution for alleged whistleblower reprisal. Under this law, OSC bears the burden of proving that protected activities or disclosures by a subordinate employee were a "significant factor" in the supervisor's decision to take the action that is alleged to be retaliatory; *see Special Counsel v. Eidmann,* 49 M.S.P.R. 614 (1991), *aff'd, Eidmann v. MSPB,* 976 F.2d 1400 (Fed. Cir. 1992); *Special Counsel v. Santella,* 65 M.S.P.R. 452 (1994). This standard is more protective of supervisors than the burden of proof applicable to employee affirmative defense or corrective action cases that also concern whistleblower reprisal. The standard in these other cases requires OSC or an employee to show merely that protected activities or disclosures were a "contributing factor" in triggering reprisal.

One additional note about OSC prosecutions is in order. The Comptroller General has ruled that an agency may pay an employee's attorney's fees related to an OSC investigation and prosecution if the employee's agency determines that the federal employee under prosecution by the OSC was acting within the scope of his employment at the time the acts complained about were committed; *see Matter of Jeannette E. Nichols,* 67 Comp. Gen. 37 (1987). If, in adjudicating the OSC complaint, the MSPB rules against the employee the agency's payment of attorney's fees cannot continue if the employee appeals the MSPB decision to federal court.

In 1994, Congress amended the WPA to permit a supervisor who successfully defends against an OSC prosecution of an alleged prohibited personnel practice to collect attorney's fees from the government.

Grievances

OPM requires all agencies to have grievance procedures by which employees can raise complaints and have them considered by higher-level management.

Federal agencies are required to have grievance procedures through which employees may raise complaints about employment problems. In many agencies these grievance procedures are negotiated formally with a labor union. Even in the absence of such a negotiated grievance procedure, OPM requires all agencies to have grievance procedures by which employees can raise complaints and have them considered by higher-level management. (5 C.F.R. Part 771)

In many instances, employees will file complaints against their supervisor alleging inappropriate supervisory conduct. Through the grievance process, the employee may ask that his supervisor be disciplined or that the manager or supervisor apologize to him. This type of relief is inappropriate and should not be granted by the agency unless it is independently determined that an apology or discipline is warranted. The employee has no right to force the agency to apologize if a grievance is not satisfactorily resolved through the informal stages of processing.

With respect to the agency grievance procedure, no outside arbitration is usually provided. Thus, the agency has discretion over the decision on the grievance. With respect to a negotiated grievance procedure, however, the labor union may take the grievance to arbitration. The arbitration is conducted in an informal hearing fashion before an arbitrator empowered to make a binding decision about the matter being grieved.

With one recent exception, arbitrators may not actually order a supervisor to be disciplined or to apologize as a result of an employee grievance. Instead, assuming the arbitrator rules in favor of the employee, an arbitrator's remedy is much more likely to focus on how the employee can be made whole and what the agency should do to remedy a wrong that was done to an employee. Of course, if as a result of the grievance process the agency learns that a supervisor acted inappropriately, the agency could discipline the supervisor. A recent change to the Whistleblower Protection Act appears to give arbitrators the authority to order discipline for supervisors who commit prohibited personnel practices. (5 U.S.C. 7121(b)(2)(A)(ii)) Of course, the supervisor could appeal such an arbitrator-ordered action to the MSPB if it results in a penalty greater than a 14-day suspension.

Thus, some risk to the supervisor is certainly present within an agency grievance system. However, the threat of disciplinary action or other employment problems resulting for the supervisor is, for all practical purposes, no greater through the exercise of grievance rights, than it would be if an employee otherwise complained and asked an agency to consider disciplining a supervisor. Short of outrageous conduct by a supervisor or obvious and intentional violations of employee rights, most supervisors have little to fear by fully co-operating through the grievance process.

MSPB And EEOC

Employees who are subjected to disciplinary action and who believe they have been discriminated against may have their cases adjudicated by either the MSPB or the Equal Employment Opportunity Commission (EEOC), subject to the jurisdictional requirements of those two agencies. The jurisdiction of the MSPB is set forth in 5 C.F.R. 1201.2 and 1201.3; the jurisdiction of the EEOC can be found in 29 C.F.R. Parts 1613 and 1614. The MSPB's procedures are examined in Chapter 21.

As part of the MSPB or EEOC process, a supervisor may be asked to testify and justify supervisory actions against an employee, but federal supervisors and managers need not fear either the EEOC or MSPB process.

Ordinarily agency attorneys or other qualified personnel officials will represent the agency at the MSPB or the EEOC, and the agency representative will usually prepare the manager or supervisor who is required to testify at the hearing. The manager or supervisor should ask the agency representative to explain the issues, and the agency representative should likewise ensure that all aspects of the employee's challenge to supervisory authority are well understood. The best way for a manager to proceed at the MSPB and the EEOC is with a straightforward, honest approach. (See Chapter 22 for a more detailed discussion of how to handle being a witness at a hearing.)

Except for Special Counsel prosecutions, neither the MSPB nor the EEOC has the authority to order that any personnel action be taken against a manager or supervisor as a result of an employee appeal. Thus, the only negative effect that could occur directly from an MSPB or EEOC decision is that the employment action will be reversed or the employee will be reinstated or otherwise made whole. If the manager or supervisor of an employee who prevails in a MSPB or EEOC case subsequently and willfully refuses to carry out a MSPB or EEOC order, the manager or supervisor could be subject to some disciplinary or other enforcement action. Only unwise supervisors would take such a defiant stand, however.

Employees subjected to disciplinary action may have their cases adjudicated by either the MSPB or EEOC.

Privacy Act

The manager or supervisor who is not careful about respecting the privacy of a subordinate employee may be subject to liability for administrative or criminal action under the Privacy Act. (5 U.S.C. 552(a)) An individual, who willfully violates the Privacy Act by disclosing without authority private information about an employee contained in an agency record, may be *criminally* prosecuted. An employee who brings a civil action in U.S. Dis-

Lawsuits From Employees

Generally, managers and supervisors who act within the scope of their employement are absolutely immune from a lawsuit by a subordinate employee.

trict Court under the Privacy Act may be entitled to recover damages and attorney's fees if information was improperly disclosed. While a complaint under the Privacy Act is not brought directly against a supervisor, the supervisor's actions of disclosing private information could be subject to scrutiny. If a supervisor has any doubt about whether private information or other information about a federal employee contained in an agency record can be released, the supervisor should promptly obtain expert advice from the Office of General Counsel or from those agency individuals who are responsible for administering Freedom of Information Act/Privacy Act requests. Providing accurate information about an employee in cases of outside employment references, however, is allowed and is protected; *see Siegert v. Gilley,* 111 S.Ct. 1789 (1991).

One of the most frequently-asked questions by supervisors concerns whether a subordinate employee can sue the supervisor in court for monetary damages. *As a general rule, managers and supervisors who act within the scope of their employment are absolutely immune from a lawsuit by a subordinate employee; see Westfall v. Erwin,* 484 U.S. 292 (1988); *Barr v. Matteo,* 360 U.S. 564 (1959). This means that any lawsuit brought against a manager or supervisor who is acting in an official capacity will in all probability be summarily dismissed. Ordinarily, the dismissal occurs without cost or undue aggravation to the supervisor, and is handled by the agency counsel and Department of Justice attorneys.

A supervisor's receipt of a lawsuit filed against him should be reported immediately to the agency's Office of General Counsel. In most instances, the agency will refer the matter to the Department of Justice, which will then enter an appearance in federal court, represent the manager or supervisor, and move for dismissal. Many such lawsuits are filed each year by disgruntled federal employees who have lost their jobs and who are, without benefit of competent legal counsel, pursuing some redress.

These cases are routinely dismissed by the federal courts with Department of Justice representation.

Also, as a general rule, employees may not sue their supervisors or others on matters arising out of the employer-employee relationship for violation of their constitutional rights; *see Bush v. Lucas,* 462 U.S. 367 (1983). However, allegations by former employees that their constitutional rights have been violated by some action arising after employment could form the subject of a constitutional tort challenge. A qualified immunity defense, and a showing of good faith on the part of the supervisor, should be sufficient to have the case dismissed.

Possible constitutional tort challenges from former employees could result from unlawful searches and seizures of property. The Supreme Court has ruled, however, that a federal supervisor's derogatory reference concerning a former employee's federal job performance did not deprive the former employee of his constitutional right to liberty and thus dismissed the former employee's lawsuit against the supervisor; *see Siegert v. Gilley,* 111 S.Ct. 1789 (1991). The Court in *Siegert* left open the issue of whether the supervisor could be sued for the tort of defamation of character. Again, the Department of Justice will ordinarily provide legal representation for constitutional torts involving former employees.

The individual liability of a federal supervisor or manager in a lawsuit filed by an employee or former employee is one of the more complex areas of federal personnel law. However, it is important for a manager or supervisor to remember that successful lawsuits by employees or former employees are exceedingly rare and usually concern allegations of sexual harassment or physical assault by a supervisor.

At the same time, however, the MSPB has upheld a subordinate employee's removal for defamatory, derogatory comments about a supervisor made outside of any protected forums, such as a grievance or EEO complaint proceeding; *see Johnson v. Dep't. of the Army,* 48 M.S.P.R. 54 (1991), *aff'd,* 960 F.2d 156 (Fed. Cir. 1992).

Summary Of Supervisory Exposure

In summary, federal managers or supervisors should remember that a properly motivated, appropriately documented, and properly processed personnel action against a subordinate federal employee will seldom result in the supervisor's personal exposure to liability. This chapter has discussed common ways that subordinate employees challenge supervisory authority. When a supervisor acts in bad faith, is careless about following rules or regulations, or fails to use good common sense about respecting the rights and dignity of a subordinate federal employee, an employee's challenge could pose more of a threat. A supervisor acting in good faith for proper reasons, however, has little reason to be concerned.

Chapter 20

The Office Of Government Ethics

Chapter 19

The Office Of Government Ethics

INTRODUCTION

Effective February 3, 1993, the Office Of Government Ethics (OGE) issued comprehensive federal employment ethics regulations. (5 C.F.R. Part 2635) These regulations are designed to supersede older regulations found at 5 C.F.R. 735.401 et seq. (Statements of Employment and Financial Interests); 5 C.F.R. Part 2634 (Financial Disclosure Requirements); 5 C.F.R. Part 2326 (Limitations on Outside Employment and Prohibition of honoraria); and Parts 2637 and 2641 (Post-Employment Conflict of Interest).

The rules cover seven areas of federal employee behavior: 1) gifts from sources outside the government; 2) gifts between government employees; 3) conflicting financial interests; 4) impartiality in performing official duties; 5) seeking other employment; 6) misuse of a government position, and 7) outside activities. The rules specifically interpret criminal statutes prohibiting or restricting private sector employment following federal employment, financial conflicts of interest, and the supplementing of a federal employee's income by outside sources. These criminal statutes can be found at 18 U.S.C. 207 through 209.

When answering questions from subordinate employees about ethics issues, supervisors should refer employees to a Designated Agency Ethics Official (DAEO). This is especially recommended in light of the intricacy and complexity of the OGE regulations.

One much-publicized issue deliberately left unregulated by OGE is the question of federal employee participation in professional associations. OGE does not have any immediate plans to regulate participation in associations. Employee use of government property, facilities, and official time for participation in professional associations could be problematic.

Gifts From Outside Sources

Return it, pay for it or share it with others.

The purpose of the outside gift rules is to prevent not only outright favoritism, but also the appearance of bias toward select members of the public. Only very modest, customary, personal, or infrequent gifts are excluded from the general prohibition against the acceptance of gifts. The regulations define the term "gift" and describe the "prohibited sources" from whom employees normally should not accept gifts. In general, employees may accept gifts having a market value of $20 or less per occasion, as long as the yearly sum of these gifts does not exceed $50. The OGE regulation includes a list of exceptions to the general prohibition against receiving gifts, even from prohibited sources. These exceptions include the $20 and $50 limits, gifts based on personal relationships, discounts available to many government employees, awards or honorary degrees, gifts based on allowable outside business or employment relationships, and expenses involved with attending widely-attended gatherings or events, such as speeches, that are in the interest of the agency. The OGE regulations even explain the proper alternative courses of action to take when an employee realizes he or she has received an improper gift: return it, pay for it or share it with others. (5 C.F.R. 2635.201)

Gifts Between Employees

Rules on gifts from employees is to prevent favoritism within the merit system.

The purpose of the rules on gifts from other employees is to prevent favoritism, or the appearance thereof, within the merit system. The rules apply strictly to those in a supervisory relationship, but do not apply to infrequent, token or voluntary gifts. Other general exceptions to the rule against accepting gifts from or giving gifts to subordinates include occasional gifts valued at less than $10 each, office-wide refreshments, and ordinary personal hospitality at an employee's residence. (5 C.F.R. 2635.301)

☑ CASE IN POINT

Brenda, a supervisor at the Agency for International Development, has just been reassigned from Washington, D.C., to Kabul, Afghanistan. For a farewell party, 12 of Brenda's subordinates have decided to take her out to lunch at the Khyber Repast. It is understood that each employee will pay for their own meal and that the cost of Brenda's lunch will be divided equally among them. The amount each subordinate will contribute to the gift cannot be determined until after Brenda has selected and ordered her lunch. Whether Brenda's subordinates may buy lunch for her, and, whether Brenda may accept lunch, depends on several factors: Are the employees in a supervisor-subordinate relationship? Will the amount of each employee's contribution be determined voluntarily? Is there a highly personal relationship involved? Is the occasion regular or infrequent?

In Brenda's case, there is clearly a supervisory relationship that will bar the gift unless it falls within one of the rule's specific exceptions. Also, the amount of the gift appears involuntary, since the subordinates are not free to choose exactly how much they will contribute, and there is no personal relationship involved that might automatically render the gift appropriate. However, the existence of a supervisory-subordinate relationship in Brenda's case is offset by two exceptions in the OGE rules: the infrequency exception and the voluntary contribution exception. The exact amount of each employee's contribution, although unknown until after Brenda orders, is considered essentially knowable, and the decision to attend and contribute to the luncheon is strictly voluntary. Also, the occasion of the luncheon is certainly infrequent and probably unique.

Conflicting Financial Interests

The OGE financial conflict rules are similar to agency-generated rules previously in place. Their purpose is to prevent the appearance of impropriety where federal employees find that their official duties may affect their private investments. (See discussion in Chapter 4 and 5 C.F.R. 2635.401.)

Impartiality In Performing Official Duties

The purpose of the impartiality rules is to prevent the appearance of impropriety in a federal employee's personal and business relationships outside the government, which might lead to bias or favoritism in the performance of official duties. Only certain "covered relationships" are subject to scrutiny, and a DAEO may approve even a covered relationship. Also note: if a newly-hired federal employee receives anything valued in excess of $10,000 from a previous employer just prior to entering government (unless pursuant to an established severance pay program), the employee will be disqualified from working on any *matter* involving the prior employer for two years following receipt of the payment. (5 C.F.R. 2635.501)

Seeking Other Employment

The rules that address seeking outside employment are designed to prevent the appearance of a personal bias in favor of specific private sector entities with whom a future employment relationship is either sought or arranged. As with the impartiality rules, a DAEO may either: 1) approve, or 2) disqualify a federal employee from participating in any action or matter, if that employee has been seeking employment with a company involved in that matter. (5 C.F.R. 2635.601).

Misuse Of Position

The purpose of misuse rules is to prevent unauthorized personal or private gain from government service or position.

The misuse rules deal with highly specific circumstances involving the use of an official title, government property, non-public information, and official time. The purpose is to prevent unauthorized personal or private gain from government service or position. The misuse of position rules cover a much broader range of conduct and should be distinguished from the misuse of government property rules discussed in Chapter 4.

☑ CASE IN POINT

Farrah, a supervisor at the Department of the Treasury, is asked to provide a letter of recommendation for a personal friend who is seeking federal employment. Farrah agrees to provide a letter of recommendation on office stationery, signed with her official title. Farrah's secretary, who is also a friend of the prospective employee, offers to type the letter at home during non-duty hours. Are Farrah and her secretary misusing their government positions? Is the use of stationery in this case a misuse of "government property?" Is Farrah's signing with her official title a misuse of her "position?" Is Farrah's secretary being required to use her personal time rather than official time? Is Farrah's secretary's offer to type the letter an improper "gift" to Farrah?

Under the OGE rules, a supervisor may use office stationery and sign with her title when drafting a letter of recommendation for either a federal employee she knows or a prospective federal employee she knows. The rules do not allow a superior to direct a secretary to type personal correspondence on official time. However, the letter of recommendation in the above case is not strictly personal, since what a federal supervisor has to say about a prospective federal employee is of genuine interest to the government.

Where a secretary's offer to type personal correspondence at home is entirely voluntary, it is allowed, unless the compensation offered is inappropriate. In the example above, no compensation was offered, *which means* the services of the supervisor's secretary were provided as a gift to the supervisor in violation of the OGE gift rules. Farrah probably should direct her secretary to type the letter at work on official time, since only where a letter of recommendation is for a non-federal employee seeking a non-federal position is there a clear violation of the rule against using stationery and signing one's official title. (5 C.F.R. 2635.701).

☑ CASE IN POINT

John is the president of a company who exports its product overseas and has applied for a license from the Department of Commerce to export these goods. John knows that his friend Bob works for the Department of Commerce and asks Bob whether he would look into why John's export license has been delayed. During a department-wide staff meeting, Bob raises the delay as a matter of official inquiry and asked that the processing of the license be expedited. Bob has used his official position in an attempt to benefit his friend and, in acting as his friend's agent for the purpose of pursuing the export license with the Department of Commerce, may also have violated the ethics provision found at 18 U.S.C. 205.

Under the rules, a government employee may not use his or her position to benefit a friend or relative's interest. The employee is also generally prohibited from endorsing any product or service by using his or her title or position. For example, the Commissioner of the Consumer Product Safety Commission may not agree to do a commercial in which she endorses an electrical appliance as being safe for residential use. Likewise, an Assistant Attorney General may not endorse a crime novel by using or referring to his official position. There are circumstances, however, where an employee's actions may not be considered an impermissible endorsement.

☑ CASE IN POINT

Joan, a Foreign Commercial Service officer from the Department of Commerce is asked by a United States telecommunications company to meet with a representative from the Spanish Government, which is in the process of procuring telecommunications services. As part of her official duties, Joan may meet with the Spanish representative and explain the advantages of procuring these services from the United States firm, as opposed to the other European companies which are also competing for the bid. This activity is within Joan's official duties because the statutory mission of the Department of Commerce includes assisting the export activities of U.S. companies.

The determination of whether an act is an "endorsement" or whether an endorsement may fall within an employee's official duties may not always be clear. An employee should therefore obtain the opinion of the agency's ethics officer whenever there is such a doubt.

> Under the rules, a government employee may not use his or her position to benefit a friend or relative's interest.
>
> He also may not endorse any product or service using his title or position.

The ethics rules also prohibit an employee from using nonpublic information to engage in financial transactions. Likewise, an employee may not use government property for unauthorized purposes.

☑ CASE IN POINT
Sally, an employee of the Department of the Navy, learns that a corporation has just won a large contract with the Department. Before this information is announced to the public, Sally tells her brother, who increases his investment in that corporation. By giving her brother this information, Sally may have violated the ethics rules.

☑ CASE IN POINT
Brian, an employee of the Commodity Futures Trading Commission, has access to a commercial service through his computer at work which provides investment information. Brian may not use the commercial service to obtain advice about his own investments.

Outside Activities

The regulations generally ban employees from receiving honoraria for any speaking appearance.

The outside activities rule covers extracurricular behavior that could conflict with the duties of a federal employee. Regulated activities include holding an outside job, giving speeches, serving as an expert witness, teaching, writing, and engaging in fund raising. One of the more controversial restrictions on outside activities is the ban on receiving honoraria for certain speaking appearances. (5 C.F.R. 2636.201 through 2636.205)

The regulations generally ban employees from receiving honoraria for any speaking appearance, including those that are completely unrelated to the employee's job duties. The Supreme Court, however, ruled in 1995 that these regulations are unconstitutional in part. Specifically, the Supreme Court found that the restriction, as it applied to employees at the GS-15 level and below, unduly restricted the first amendment rights of employees who wished to speak on topics unrelated to their job duties. The full restriction continues to apply, however, to employees at or above the GS-15 level or in the senior executive service.

In general, the OGE rules prohibit payment for:

1) speeches or lectures related to one's work duties given outside the context of an accredited educational institution;

2) articles and books that address the specifics of the employee's work, revealing nonpublic information;

3) misusing the employee's official title as an advertisement or false endorsement by the government;

4) reproducing knowledge gleaned from government service for a profit;

5) serving as an expert trial witness (except on behalf of the government) in any case where the government is a party or has a substantial interest;

6) holding an outside job or engaging in outside activities that might present the appearance of a conflict of interest with the employee's government work; and

7) certain fund-raising activities; such as the Hatch Act prohibitions against engaging in certain partisan political activities. (5 U.S.C. 7321-7328).

Nonetheless, the rules allow many of these same activities if, depending on circumstances, the agency gives prior approval. Also, note that the rules specifically do not address some ethical issues surrounding an employee's decision to participate in a professional association, instead, referring employees to existing guidance in the Federal Personnel Manual.

Ethics Rules That Apply To Contractors Under The Federal Acquisition Regulations

Apart from the ethics regulations promulgated by the Office of Government Ethics, there are guidelines in the Federal Acquisition Regulations that govern the business practices of agencies and their contractors. Chapter 1, part 3, Title 48 of the Code of Federal Regulations generally states that any conflict of interest or the appearance of a conflict of interest shall be avoided in government-contractor relationships.

These regulations specifically prohibit a government employee from soliciting or accepting any gratuity, gift, favor, entertainment, loan or anything else of value from a government contractor or from a business that seeks to become a government contractor. (48 C.F.R. 3.101-2) They also provide specific rules for procurement officers. (48 C.F.R. 3.104-3) During the conduct of any procurement of property or services, procurement officials are prohibited from soliciting or accepting future employment from the competing contractor, soliciting or accepting, directly or indirectly, anything of value from a competing contractor, and disclosing any proprietary or source selection information regarding the procurement other than to the authorized contracting officer.

☑ CASE IN POINT

Alison works as a procurement officer at the Department of Commerce, but is thinking about leaving the Department because she has heard that she can get paid more from a private firm. As part of her job at the Department of Commerce, Alison is presently trying to procure rubber bands because a shortage has arisen. ACME Corporation is a company which specializes in manufacturing office supplies, including rubber bands. During one of her conversations with Mike, who is the contracting officer for ACME Corporation, he mentions that a position is opening up in their procurement department. Alison hints to Mike that she would be interested and Mike tells her to forward her resume to Sally, the corporation's hiring specialist. Alison's conduct could be considered as a solicitation of future employment from ACME. Alison should not have indicated she was interested in the job; rather, she should wait until after the contractor selection has been made. Further, once Alison has applied for the job, she should abstain from being involved with any procurements where ACME is a competing contractor. If Alison is then hired by ACME, Alison must abstain for two years from being involved in any matter involving the contract she participated in awarding ACME while working for the Department. (48 C.F.R. 3.104-6, 3.104-7, 3.104(d))

Conclusion

New OGE rules cover a broader range of conduct and are uniform from agency to agency.

Violations of any of the above ethical obligations could result in disciplinary action, removal, civil fines, or even criminal penalties. The new OGE rules cover a broader range of detailed conduct than their predecessors, which, while perhaps more restrictive of employee behavior, has the advantage of uniformity from agency to agency, something the prior agency specific regulations lacked. Under the OGE rules, agencies can still promulgate their own unique sets of regulations (*see, e.g.,* 5 C.F.R. 3101 et seq.), but if they choose to do so, they now must first obtain OGE approval. In the short term, the OGE rules may confuse federal employees and keep DAEO's busy answering questions. Supervisors should be sensitive to the initial confusion and refer employees to a DAEO whenever potential problems arise.

The Merit Systems Protection Board

The Merit Systems Protection Board

THE STRUCTURE OF THE MSPB

The MSPB, or Board, is an independent government agency, which operates somewhat like a court. One of its primary functions is to adjudicate the appeals of federal employees in cases where an agency has taken an adverse action against the employee based on misconduct or performance.

The Board has three members, each of whom is appointed by the President and confirmed by the Senate. Each Member serves a seven-year term. The Board also has a staff to assist it in accomplishing its various regional offices across the United States. The first step in the appeals process after an employee files an appeal form is an evidentiary hearing, which is conducted by an administrative judge in one of the various regional offices. After the hearing and a decision by an administrative judge, either party can appeal to the three-member board for a final decision. If neither party appeals, the administrative judge's decision will become final 35 days after it is issued.

Notice Of MSPB Appeal Rights

The MSPB hears appeals from many types of agency actions, including reductions in grade, removals for unacceptable performance or misconduct, and suspension of more than 14 days. When an agency issues a decision adverse to an employee, the agency must advise the employee whether the matter may be appealed to the MSPB. If the employee has MSPB appeal rights, the agency must advise the employee of any time limits for appealing to the Board, as well as the address of the appropriate Board office where the appeal must be filed. Under current regulations, an employee is required to file an appeal with the Board no later than 30 days after the effective date of the appealable action. The agency must also provide the employee a copy (or access to a copy) of the Board's regulations and a copy of the appeal form which the employee can use. The employee should also be told whether he has the right to file a grievance or an EEO complaint.

Agency Response To The Appeal (The Agency File)

An employee appeal initiates the agency's response. The agency's response must include (among other things) all evidence relied upon by the agency to support its adverse action against the employee. (5 U.S.C. 7513(e)) This evidence and documentation will become a part of the administrative appeal file. The agency must also provide a statement setting forth the agency action against the employee and its reasons for taking the action.

The agency's appeal file, or agency file as it is called by the MSPB, is a critical document. It is the first impression the agency makes upon the administrative judge who will decide the employee's appeal. A well-documented agency file that appears to be objective will make a favorable impression. On the other hand, an agency file that appears to be incomplete or biased may indicate to the administrative judge that the agency had some improper motive for taking the action. These first impressions are important and the supervisor/manager must ensure that the agency file presents the most favorable impression possible.

Right To Representation, Use Of Witnesses And Discovery

Both the agency and the employee have the right to have an attorney or other representative at the MSPB. The employee and the agency also have the right to call witnesses to testify on their behalf at the hearing.

If the witness is a federal employee, the witness is in an official duty status when he appears to testify. Therefore, he is not entitled to a fee for appearing as a witness. The federal employee witness is, however, entitled to pay and benefits, including travel and per diem if appropriate.

If the witness is not a federal employee, he is entitled to the same fee and mileage allowances paid to witnesses who are subpoenaed to testify in federal courts.

Both the agency and the employee are permitted to conduct "discovery" prior to the hearing. Discovery is a process by which either party may obtain any information that the other party has that may have a bearing on the outcome of the case. The discovery process may be used to uncover relevant documents either side may wish to introduce at the hearing, as well as the identity of all witnesses each party intends to call at the hearing.

If a supervisor/manager is called to testify at a deposition (a question-and-answer session) by an employee's attorney, he should prepare as he would for the hearing itself. A deposition is a tool available to either side during discovery in which witnesses appear, usually at the offices of the attorney taking the deposition, and answer questions under oath. A stenographer is present and transcribes the answers. Anything said in the deposition can become a part of the record of the hearing itself and can also be used to "impeach," or challenge, a supervisor's or manager's later testimony if their hearing testimony is inconsistent with statements made in the deposition. The deposition should not be taken lightly and care should be taken to assure that the testimony is complete and consistent at both the deposition and the hearing. If you are going to testify at a deposition, be sure to consult with the agency attorney prior to the session.

> Both the agency and the employee have the right to representation, to call witnesses in their behalf and to conduct discovery.

The Evidentiary Hearing Before The Administrative Judge

Most MSPB hearings take place about two months after the appeal is filed. Typically, a week or two before the hearing, the parties must identify the witnesses they expect to call, and must clearly define the issues to be adjudicated in the hearing. The evidentiary hearing before the administrative judge is normally open to the public, as are most trials in federal and state courts. The administrative judge may, however, order a hearing closed when in the best interest of a particular witness, the public or the employee. Because public hearings provide a check on the lawful operation of the federal government, hearings will generally not be closed based solely on the interests of the agency.

A verbatim transcript of the hearing is recorded to preserve the substance of the hearing in the event either party appeals the decision.

The Decision Of The Administrative Judge

After both the agency and the employee have presented their cases, including the presentation of all relevant documents, evidence and testimony of witnesses, the administrative judge issues an Initial Decision addressing all issues presented by the parties. The Initial Decision becomes final 35 days after it is issued unless either party files a Petition for Review with the full MSPB in Washington, D.C. If appealed to the full Board, the Initial Decision may be affirmed, reversed, modified or vacated in whole or in part.

The current policy of the MSPB is to issue an Initial Decision within 120 days of the filing of the appeal. The requirement is nearly always met by the administrative judges. In some situations where more than 120 days is needed by the employee, or for other legitimate reasons, an appeal may be dismissed without prejudice by the administrative judge subject to being refiled by the employee at a later date.

Compared to other litigating forums, the MSPB operates quickly. A decision within 120 days (about four months), including a period for discovery and a hearing, is very rapid in the American legal system, so the agency should be prepared to try the case at the time it issues the decision on the adverse action. In fact, being able to control the timing of the effective date of the adverse action places the agency at a significant advantage in preparation for an MSPB case. For example, the agency may issue a removal decision with an effective date 14 days from the date of issuance in order to ensure that the deciding official will have ample opportunity to consult with agency counsel or the personnel office for the purpose of preparing for a likely MSPB appeal.

Appeals

A final decision of the full MSPB may be appealed to the United States Court of Appeals for the Federal Circuit.

Attorneys Fees And Expenses

If the employee prevails against the agency at the MSPB, both the administrative judge and the full Board have statutory authority to order the agency to reimburse the employee for reasonable attorney fees and expenses incurred by the employee in appealing the adverse action to the MSPB. If fees are awarded, they are paid out of the agency's budget. This is also true if the employee prevails at the appellate level in the U.S. Court of Appeals for the Federal Circuit.

What To Do When Called As A Witness At A Hearing

What To Do When Called As A Witness

Administrative Hearings And Trials

A witness should treat an arbitration hearing with the same dignity and respect as he would a court proceding.

Discovery

At some point during a career in the federal government, a supervisor or manager may be called to testify at a hearing. This may arise where the agency has taken an adverse action against an employee, and the employee has either appealed the matter to arbitration or the Merit Systems Protection Board (MSPB), or the employee has filed an EEO complaint that is being adjudicated by the Equal Employment Opportunity Commission (EEOC) or in court.

A supervisor or manager may be requested to appear as a witness at a trial or administrative hearing. Although an administrative hearing is quite similar to a courtroom trial, it is somewhat less formal. State or federal court trials may involve a jury, but in an MSPB hearing or EEOC hearing, the administrative judge makes the decisions instead of a jury. There are, however, many similarities. A judge presides over the MSPB or EEOC hearing, just as a judge supervises a federal or state trial. The MSPB and EEOC judge also considers the sworn testimony of witnesses who have first-hand knowledge of information concerning the case he is deciding.

In an arbitration, much the same rules will apply as in other administrative hearings. An arbitration is a somewhat less formal proceeding, however, and may be held in the agency's conference room or a similar facility. An arbitrator is generally an expert in labor law who has been selected to hear the case by agreement of both parties. In contrast to an MSPB or court trial case, there will not be depositions, interrogatories, or requests for documents with which to comply unless the agency and the union have agreed to allow these types of discovery. When testifying in an arbitration, a witness will be required to take an oath to tell the truth, just as in an MSPB or EEOC hearing.

Remember, this is a serious matter, and a witness should treat an arbitration hearing with the same dignity and respect as he would a court proceeding.

Agency managers and supervisors who have personal knowledge of facts being decided by the judge, or who are knowledgeable about agency practices in general (such as a personnel specialist), may be called to testify as witnesses at an administrative hearing, arbitration, or trial. Prior to testifying, the witness should meet with the agency attorney or labor relations specialist handling the matter and be prepared to give testimony. Preparation is essential, both to ensure that important information is provided through the witness' testimony, as well as to allow the witness to understand what the case is about and to understand how his testimony fits in with the rest of the agency's case.

Discovery is a process in information gathering used by both sides in a case. Discovery includes depositions, interrogatories, requests for documents and so forth. (5 C.F.R. 1201.71-1201.85) In a deposition, one side subpoenas (obtains an order to compel attendance) a witness from the other side and questions the witness before a court reporter. This occurs before a hearing, and no judge is present. The attorneys for both sides attend the deposition. The purpose of a deposition is to "discover" the facts known by witnesses for the other side before a trial or hearing, to the extent possible, so that there are no surprises during the hearing.

If a supervisor or manager is required to appear at a deposition, it is essential that he be prepared for it by the agency counsel and that the witness testify in the same manner as he would if actually testifying at the hearing.

Testimony at a deposition is under oath, just as it is in a trial or hearing, and the transcript may be used at trial to attack the credibility of (impeach) a witness who testifies inconsistently with prior sworn testimony.

Interrogatories are written requests sent from one side to the other side's attorney asking for documents and information about the case. A supervisor may be required to help the agency attorney prepare answers to interrogatories and may be required to sign the interrogatory responses to attest to the validity of the answers provided to opposing counsel. Requests for documents are usually sent with interrogatories. Documents requested must be provided to the other side unless they are not relevant or are privileged. The agency attorney will decide what must be sent. However, as with interrogatories, the supervisor or manager may be required to attest to the validity of documents provided.

> Discovery includes depositions, interrogatories and request for documents.

Truthful Testimony

It is essential that each person who is called as a witness in a hearing or in a deposition tell the truth. Even if the testimony of an agency manager may help the employee's case and hurt the agency's case, the manager must testify truthfully so that the judge can base his decision on an accurate record of what happened between the agency and the employee. If the supervisor or manager believes his testimony will harm the agency's case, he may wish to recommend to the agency attorney that he settle the case.

Visit The Setting Where The Incident Occurred

If a witness in a case is to testify about an incident he personally observed, the witness should try to revisit the physical setting before the hearing. While visiting the setting, he may find it helpful to close his eyes, and try to picture the scene, the people who were there, how far apart the people were and what was said.

Witness

Appearance And Conduct

At the hearing, the witness should wear the clothes he would normally wear when he is representing the agency before the public. For example, if the witness would normally wear a coat and tie at work, it would be inappropriate for him to appear at the hearing dressed in jeans and tennis shoes. The witness should be serious at all times during the hearing itself. He should avoid laughing and talking about the case in common areas in the building where the hearing is conducted, including the halls, entrances and restrooms. The witness should not chew gum or smoke while testifying. He should conduct himself in a dignified manner when taking the oath that he will tell the truth, the whole truth and nothing but the truth. The witness should stand upright, with good posture, while he is taking the oath. As the oath is important, the witness should pay close attention to the words he repeats and say them clearly.

Use A Natural Tone When Testifying

The witness should answer questions naturally and truthfully.

The witness should not try to memorize the testimony he gives at the hearing. Rather, he should listen to the questions that are asked of him and answer them naturally and truthfully.

If the judge asks the witness questions, the witness should answer naturally. If possible, the witness should establish eye contact with the judge and speak as he would to any supervisor or peer.

A court reporter will be recording or transcribing every word that is spoken during the hearing in order to prepare a written transcript of the case. The witness should speak clearly and loudly enough so that the court reporter, the lawyers and the judge can easily hear what the witness is saying. The witness should respond to questions with a "yes" or a "no" answer rather than a nod or shake of the head so that the court reporter can hear and transcribe the answer. The witness should try to minimize nervous habits, such as talking with his hand over his mouth or chewing gum.

Responding To Questions

The witness will be questioned by attorneys for the agency and for the employee. After the agency's attorneys have asked all of their questions of the witness during the direct examination, the employee's attorney will have an opportunity to conduct a cross examination of the witness. This means that the employee's attorney will ask the witness questions in order to obtain information that may help the employee's case. The witness should remember at all times that the cross-examining attorney may try to make the witness look bad so that the judge will not believe the witness' testimony. Since each attorney has a different technique for conducting a cross examination, it is impossible to prepare a strategy for predicting the exact questions the attorneys may ask. Thus, the best strategy is to listen carefully to the questions asked and try to respond briefly and truthfully.

If the witness mistakenly gives an answer that is incorrect during the direct or cross examination, and realizes his mistake while he is still on the stand, the witness should correct the mistake immediately. Similarly, the witness may explain his answers where necessary. If a question is somewhat misleading, and if it cannot be answered with a simple "yes" or "no," the witness has a right to explain his answer more fully.

Some attorneys may try to trick the witness into losing his temper or saying things that are incorrect. For this reason it is important for the witness to remain calm throughout the cross examination by keeping responses direct, short and truthful. A witness should not pause after each question to try to figure out whether his response will help or hurt the agency's case. The witness should, however, avoid blurting out responses without first making sure that he understands the question.

As a general rule, the witness should answer each question directly. This means that he should respond only to the question that is asked of him and then stop talking. The witness should not volunteer any information that is not specifically asked for by one of the attorneys. Thus, the witness should concentrate on responding as concisely as possible to the precise question asked. The witness should avoid "making up" answers. Responding "I do not know" or "I do not remember" is a perfectly acceptable answer, so long as it is a truthful response to a question.

> The witness should avoid answering without first making sure he understands the question.

Be Polite

A witness should never argue with the attorney questioning him, even if the attorney becomes rude. If the attorney becomes rude, the judge will recognize the inappropriate behavior. Arguing with an attorney or responding in a sarcastic tone only makes the witness look bad, and may hurt the agency's case.

Answering Inappropriate Questions And Objections

During the hearing, the attorney for the agency or the employee may ask the witness questions that the witness finds inappropriate. In cases where the witness does not wish to answer a question, he should not ask the judge whether he must answer it. It is not the witness' job to object to questions.

Rather, the witness should go ahead and answer the question. If a question is improper or seeks information that is irrelevant to the case, the agency's attorney will object to the question. If an objection is made, the witness should wait until the judge has ruled on the objection before answering the question.

If the judge rules that a question is proper after an objection has been made, the witness must answer the question. If the judge rules that the question is improper, the witness will not have to answer the question.

Answering Questions Without "Hints" From Agency Attorneys

During the hearing the witness should not look at the agency's attorney or at the judge for assistance in answering a question. Often a nervous witness may look at his attorney with a facial expression that seems to say, "How should I answer this question?" Although the witness may simply be confused and trying to get clarification from his attorney, the ultimate result is that the judge will think that the witness is looking for a signal from his attorney indicating what the "right" answer is to a particular question. This can hurt the witness' credibility and suddenly make all of his otherwise truthful and helpful testimony seem questionable. If the witness does not understand a question, however, it is perfectly proper to say so, and ask that it be restated.

Responding To Questions For Specific Technical Information

If the employee's attorney asks the witness a question concerning specific information, such as the exact distance the employee traveled or the precise time that an incident occurred, the witness should provide specific information only if he knows that his response is accurate.

If the witness' response is only an estimate, he should be certain to indicate that his response is just an estimate. Prior to the hearing, the witness should discuss any matters that require detailed responses for information (such as speeds, exact words that were used during conversations, distances and time) with the agency's attorney. This will help the witness refresh his memory about what he knows, as well as inform the agency's attorney of information that may be helpful.

Conclusion Of Testimony

Once the witness completes his testimony, the judge will notify the witness that he is free to step down from the witness stand. The witness should always wait until he is excused by the judge in the event the judge or the attorneys have some additional, last minute questions to ask the witness. Once the judge excuses the witness, he should step down from the witness stand with a confident facial expression and posture. The judge will often tell the witness not to discuss his testimony with other witnesses until after the case is concluded. The witness should obey this instruction—failure to do so could be harmful to the agency's case.

Glossary

Administrative Judge - Any person authorized by the Merit Systems Protection Board (MSPB) or the Equal Employment Opportunity Commission (EEOC) to hold a hearing or to decide a case without a hearing. (5 C.F.R. 1201.4(a) and 29 C.F.R. 1614.109)

Adverse Action - An unfavorable personnel action taken by an agency against an employee, including reassignment, suspension without pay, reduction in grade or removal of the employee. (5 U.S.C. 7503 and 7513)

Affirmative Defense - Even where an agency meets the evidentiary standard (burden of proof) in proving charges against an employee, an adverse action may be overturned by the MSPB or court if the employee is able to prove certain affirmative defenses. (5 C.F.R. 1201.56(b)) Affirmative defenses are above and beyond the traditional defenses, such as a claim by the employee that he did not engage in the alleged misconduct. A common example of an affirmative defense is the existence of a handicap. Here, even if the agency proves the elements of its case against the employee, the employee may prevail using the affirmative defense that his or her handicap impacted upon the employee's performance and that the agency failed to accommodate the employee. (Additional affirmative defenses include unlawful discrimination, mistakes of law, whistleblower reprisal and so forth.) (5 U.S.C. 7701(c)(2))

Age Discrimination in Employment Act - A law enacted by Congress which promotes employment of persons over 40 years of age based on ability rather than age, and prohibits discrimination in employment based upon a person's age. (29 U.S.C. 621, et seq.)

Clear and Convincing Evidence - Describes a burden of proof (e.g., proof beyond a reasonable doubt) which a person must fulfill to prove a point in certain legal proceedings. The "clear and convincing" standard is a higher burden of proof than the standard which is required to win a case which applies a preponderance of the evidence standard. The preponderance of the evidence standard is applied by the MSPB in all adverse action cases except for performance cases, which apply the substantial evidence standard. (5 C.F.R. 1201.56(a)) When a clear and convincing standard is applied, the deciding official, judge or panel must be convinced that the agency's version of any disputed facts is correct.

Critical Element - Describes those aspects of each position which are so essential to the job that unacceptable performance of any of those particular aspects would render it impossible for the employee to perform his job effectively. (5 C.F.R. 432.103(b)) (See Noncritical Element.)

Cross Examination - Refers to the period during a formal hearing or trial when the attorney for one party asks questions of a witness who testified for the opposing party. For example, at an MSPB hearing, the employee's attorneys will conduct a cross examination of the agency's witnesses after each witness testifies for the agency. This is done in order to emphasize weaknesses in the witness' testimony or to obtain additional information that was not brought out during the direct examination of that witness. (See Direct Examination.)

Glossary

Designated Agency Ethics Official (DAEO) - The person designated by an agency to respond to ethics questions raised by agency employees, specifically questions regarding conflict of interest, gifts, and post employment restrictions.

Direct Examination - Refers to the period during a formal hearing or trial when the attorney for one party asks questions of its witnesses. (See Cross Examination).

Discovery - The process prior to hearing or trial through which both the agency and the appellant (employee), may obtain information the other party has which may have a bearing on the outcome of the case. The discovery process may be used to uncover relevant documents which either side may wish to introduce at the hearing, as well as the identity of all witnesses each party wishes to call at the hearing. (5 C.F.R. 1201.71, et seq.; 29 C.F.R. 1614.109(b)) Discovery may include the taking of depositions, requests for interrogatories, and requests for relevant documents, all from the other party to the case.

Discrimination - Unfair treatment or denial of normal privileges to persons where no reasonable distinction can be found between those favored and those not favored. Federal statutes prohibit discrimination in employment on the basis of sex, race, age, nationality, religion, and handicap. The main statutory sources of protection from discrimination in employment are Title VII of the Civil Rights Act of 1964, as amended, and the Age Discrimination in Employment Act. (See also Sexual Harassment and Handicapped Employee.)

Douglas Factors - Criteria established by the Merit Systems Protection Board to be considered by a supervisor or manager when deciding the appropriate penalty to be imposed for an employee's misconduct.

Employee Assistance Program (EAP) - A confidential program designed to assist employees in dealing with personal problems, such as alcohol or drug dependence.

Efficiency of the Service - The legal standard by which an agency may take an adverse action against an employee based on misconduct. (5 U.S.C. 7503(a) and 7513(a)) A detailed discussion of the meaning accorded to the phrase by the Merit Systems Protection Board is provided in Chapter 2.

Ex Parte Communication - Contacts by one interested participant in a legal proceeding with the person deciding the matter (usually a judge) without providing notice of the contact to the other participant. Such communications are prohibited in most forums due to the risk that the party who is excluded from the communication may be prejudiced by an information exchange between his opponent and the judge. (5 C.F.R. 1201.101(a)) In application to agency administrative proceedings, the Court of Appeals for the Federal Circuit has held that ex parte communications between the proposing official and the deciding official tainted the agency's investigation of the employee and denied the employee his constitutional right to due process; *see Sullivan v. Dep't of the Navy,* 720 F.2d 1266 (Fed. Cir. 1983).

Glossary

Final Interview - An EEO counselor should conduct a final interview with the employee no more than 30 days after the employee brings his discrimination problem to the attention of the EEO counselor. If the problem has not been resolved within the 30-day period, the EEO counselor must notify the employee in writing at the time of the final interview that the employee may file a discrimination complaint at any time up to 15 days after he receives the notice from the counselor. (29 C.F.R. 1614.105(d))

Fitness for Duty - A medical examination which an agency may require an employee or applicant for employment to undergo. The agency may only require an individual who has applied for or occupies a position which has medical standards or physical requirements to report for a medical examination prior to appointment, on a regularly recurring, periodic basis after appointment, or whenever there is a direct question about an employee's continued capacity to meet the physical or medical requirements for the position. (5 C.F.R. 339.301)

Handicapped Employee - In the federal workplace a handicapped employee in one who has, or who is regarded as having a mental or physical impairment which substantially limits one or more of the employee's major life activities, such as walking, seeing, hearing, speaking, breathing, learning, working or caring for one's self. (29 C.F.R. 1614.203) Federal statutes and regulations prohibit discrimination against handicapped employees. (29 C.F.R. 1614.203)

Harmful Procedural Error - An agency's error in the application of its procedures that is likely to have caused the agency to reach a conclusion different from the conclusion it would have reached in the absence of the error. Harmful procedural error is an affirmative defense that may typically be raised by an appellant (employee) before the MSPB. In this scenario, the burden is upon the appellant to show that the agency's error caused substantial harm or prejudice to the appellant's rights. (5 C.F.R. 1201.56(c)(3))

Indefinite suspension - A means of placing an employee in a temporary status without duties and pay pending investigation by the agency or further agency action. (5 C.F.R. 752.402(e)) An employee subject to an indefinite suspension is entitled at the earliest practicable date to notice of the reasons for the agency's action. (5 U.S.C. 7513(b) and 5 C.F.R 752.404)

Initial Decision - The judgment issued by the MSPB administrative judge after he considers all of the evidence in a case. An initial decision becomes a final decision 35 days after it is issued, unless either party files an appeal, known as a Petition for Review, with the MSPB. (5 C.F.R. 1201.113)

The MSPB may affirm, reverse, modify or vacate the entire initial decision of the administrative judge, or it may modify a portion of it. (5 C.F.R. 1201.116(b))

Glossary

Investigative File - Various documents and information acquired during the investigation of an EEO complaint, which are organized to show their relevance to the complaint or the general environment out of which the EEO complaint arose. (29 C.F.R. 1614.108 (b))

Leave Restriction Notice - A typical notice informs an employee who has taken excessive sick leave, or supplied inadequate evidence in support of leave, that sick leave will not be granted unless proper medical certification is provided. Failure to comply with such a notice may give rise to discipline.

Major Life Activities - See Handicapped Employee.

Merit Systems Protection Board (MSPB) - The MSPB is an independent government agency that operates like a court by adjudicating federal employee appeals of agency personnel actions. The MSPB was created to ensure that all federal government agencies follow federal merit system practices. (5 C.F.R. 1200.1) The MSPB consists of three, Presidentially-appointed, Senate-confirmed members. The MSPB also employs administrative judges to conduct hearings and render initial decisions in cases. The initial decisions of the MSPB administrative judges are appealable to the full MSPB through the filing of a Petition for Review. (5 C.F.R. 1201.114)

Notice Letter - A Performance Improvement Plan (PIP) - A PIP is initiated by a supervisor who provides the employee with a notice letter in which the employee is notified that his or her performance is unacceptable in one or more critical elements. The notice letter details the performance standards or requirements the employee must fulfill to demonstrate acceptable performance. The agency may also notify the employee that unless his performance in the critical element(s) improves to, and is maintained at, an acceptable level, the employee may be reduced in grade or removed. (5 C.F.R. 432.104) (See also Performance Improvement Plan.)

Noncritical Element - Those aspects of a job which are not absolutely essential to the successful completion of the employee's job but are sufficiently important to warrant evaluation on the employee's annual performance appraisal. (See Critical Element.)

Official Personnel File - A permanent file maintained by each agency containing long-term records affecting an employee's status and service as required by the Office of Personnel Management. This file is distinct from other files maintained on the employee, such as a grievance file, a drop file, or an investigative file produced as a result of an EEO complaint. (5 C.F.R. 293.301, et seq.)

Office of Government Ethics (OGE) - An executive branch agency responsible for overseeing and providing guidance on government ethics for executive branch employees and officials. (5 C.F.R. 2600.101 and 2635 et seq.)

Office of Special Counsel - The Office of Special Counsel (OSC) is an independent government agency headed by the Special Counsel. The Office of Special Counsel was created by

Congress to protect employees, former employees, and applicants for employment from prohibited personnel practices. (5 U.S.C. 1212(a))

To carry out its mission, the Office of Special Counsel may receive and investigate allegations of prohibited personnel practices and, where appropriate, bring petitions for stays and for corrective action, file complaints or make recommendations for disciplinary action. (5 U.S.C. 1212(a)(2))

Performance Improvement Plan (PIP) - The individualized plan developed by an agency to be provided to an employee whose performance in one or more critical elements has been determined to be below the fully successful level. (5 C.F.R. 432.103(e)) As part of the PIP, the agency is to notify the employee of the critical element in which he or she is performing below the fully successful level and describe the improvement that the employee must demonstrate to attain fully successful performance. The period of time during which the employee performs under the PIP is known as the Opportunity to Demonstrate Acceptable Performance. For an example of an appropriate "PIP" and a reasonable opportunity to demonstrate acceptable performance; *see Luscri v. Dep't of Army,* 39 M.S.P.R. 482 (1989).

Performance Standard - A statement of the expectations or requirements established by management for each position. (5 C.F.R. 430.203) A performance standard is required to permit the accurate evaluation of job performance on the basis of objective criteria. (5 U.S.C. 4302(b)(1)) An agency may give content to performance standards by informing an employee of specific work requirements through written instructions and other information. For a discussion of the information sufficient to provide an employee with a firm benchmark toward which to aim his performance, *see O'Neal v. Dep't of Army,* 47 M.S.P.R. 433 (1991), *see also Burroughs v. Dep't of Health and Human Services,* 49 M.S.P.R. 644 (1991). For an example of "backwards" performance standards which do not meet the requirement of permitting accurate evaluation, *see Eibel v. Dep't of Navy,* 857 F2d. 1439 (Fed. Cir. 1988).

Petition For Review - See Initial Decision.

Preponderance of the Evidence - A burden of proof which a person must fulfill to prove a point in certain legal proceedings. When a preponderance of the evidence standard is applied, as in MSPB misconduct cases, the deciding official must be convinced that a contested fact concerning the misconduct is more likely true than not. (5 C.F.R. 1201.56(c)(2)) (See Clear and Convincing Evidence, Substantial Evidence.)

Prohibited Personnel Practices - The 11 prohibitions set forth in the law at 5 U.S.C. 2302(b) with respect to persons who have authority to take, direct others to take, recommend, or approve any federal personnel action.

Persons with such authority may not engage in the activities listed in 5 U.S.C. 2302(b)(1) through (11). In cases where an employee demonstrates that a prohibited personnel prac-

Glossary

tice has been committed, an agency's adverse action may be reversed. Examples of prohibited personnel practices include terminating an employee for engaging in whistleblowing activities or retaliation if the employee exercises an appeal right, such as filing a complaint/grievance.

Qualified Handicapped Employee - A handicapped employee who, with or without a reasonable accommodation, can perform the essential functions of his or her position without endangering the health and safety of the individual or others. (29 C.F.R. 1614.203(a)(6)) (See also Handicapped Employee and Reasonable Accommodation.)

Reasonable Accommodation - The law states that each federal agency has an obligation to make "reasonable accommodation" to each qualified handicapped employee. This means, for example, that the agency must, within reason, make its physical facilities accessible to handicapped persons who are fully capable of performing the job. In addition, the agency must restructure a qualified handicapped employee's job, including adjustments to schedules, equipment and examinations, to the extent these "accommodations" or adjustments do not impose an undue hardship on the agency's overall day-to-day activities. (29 C.F.R. 1614.203(c)-(g))

Recommended Decision - In a discrimination-based case that has been appealed to the EEOC, after the administrative judge has examined all evidence in a case, the administrative judge will prepare a recommended decision. In the recommended decision, the administrative judge will explain whether he or she believes the employee has been discriminated against and, if so, what steps the agency should take to correct the problem. (29 C.F.R. 1614.109(g))

Rehabilitation Act of 1973 - A law enacted by Congress which places an affirmative obligation on the federal government to act as a model employer for the handicapped by requiring the government to seek out, hire, and accommodate qualified handicapped employees. (29 U.S.C. 791)

Report of Investigation (ROI) - A summary of the objective factual findings of the investigator assigned to investigate a formal EEO complaint. This ROI is included in the Investigative File and is used by the agency as a basis for the agency's proposed disposition of the EEO complaint.

Reprisal - An action taken by one person, either in spite of or as retaliation for, an assumed or real wrong by another. Reprisal is typically used to describe an action by a supervisor toward an employee which the employee claims was taken for other than legitimate reasons and, more specifically, because the employee engaged in protected activity such as filing a grievance or complaint or disclosing a violation of law, rule or regulation. Reprisal against an employee in these circumstances constitutes a prohibited personnel practice. (5 U.S.C. 2302(b))

Glossary

Sexual Harassment - One type of conduct which is prohibited in the federal workplace. The many different types of sexual harassment include unwelcome sexual advances, requests for sexual favors, and other verbal or physical conduct of a sexual nature when one person states or implies that the other person must submit to his or her advances as a condition of the person's continued employment, hiring or promotion. Sexual harassment also includes unwelcome advances or comments that unreasonably interfere with the individual's work performance or create an intimidating and uncomfortable atmosphere at work. (29 C.F.R. 1604.11)

Stay - A legal term for a delay in a case. The MSPB may order a stay of a personnel action if there are reasonable grounds to believe that the personnel action was taken, or is to be taken, as a result of a prohibited personnel practice. (5 U.S.C. 1214(b)(1)) If an employee requests that the MSPB "stay" the agency's adverse action and the request is granted, the agency's action will not become effective until after the MSPB has issued a decision in the employee's case.

Substantial Evidence - A burden of proof which a person must fulfill to prove a point in certain legal proceedings. Substantial evidence is that degree of relevant evidence that a reasonable person, considering the record as a whole, might accept as adequate to support a conclusion, even though other reasonable persons might disagree. Substantial evidence is a lower standard of proof than preponderance of the evidence. At the MSPB, all performance-based adverse actions must be supported by substantial evidence. (5 C.F.R. 1201.56(a)(1) and (c)(1))

Whistleblowing - An employee's disclosure of information which: 1) demonstrates that a law, rule or regulation has been violated, or 2) evidences blatant mismanagement, an excessive waste of funds, an abuse of authority or a considerable and specific danger to public health or safety. (5 U.S.C. 1213(a))

Whistleblower Protection Act of 1989 - A Law enacted by Congress which states that an employee may appeal a personnel action that the agency takes, proposes, threatens to take, or does not take as retaliation for the employee's whistleblowing activities; see Public Law 101-12, April 10, 1989. (5 U.S.C. 1221, et seq.)

FPMI Publications

PRICES EFFECTIVE THROUGH DECEMBER 31, 1997.

Shipping: 1-10 Books: $4; 11-50 Books: $12; 51+ Books: Actual UPS Shipping Rates

The Federal Manager's Handbook (3rd Ed.)	$21.95
Face To Face: A Guide for Supervisors Who Counsel Problem Employees	$12.95
The Federal Manager's Guide to Liability (2nd Ed.)	$10.95
The Federal Manager's Guide to EEO (3rd Ed.)	$10.95
Customer Service in Government	$10.95
Diversity: Straight Talk From The Trenches	$10.95
Managing Diversity: A Practical Guide	$10.95
A Practical Guide To Self-Managed Teams	$10.95
The Federal Manager's Guide To Discipline (3rd Ed.)	$10.95
Achieving Consensus	$9.95
EEO Settlements	$10.95
Understanding The Federal Retirement Systems	$9.95
How To Build An Effective Team	$10.95
RIF and the Federal Employee (2nd Ed.)	$9.95
Improving Employee Performance (2nd Ed.)	$10.95
Career Transition: A Guide for Federal Employees in a Time of Turmoil	$10.95
Performance Management: Performance Standards and You	$9.95
Dealing With Organizational Change	$6.95
EEO Today: A Guide To Understanding the EEO Process	$9.95
Managing Effectively In A Reinvented Government	$9.95
Managing The Civilian Workforce (2nd Ed.)	$9.95
The Bargaining Book (3rd Ed.)	$12.95
The Supervisor's Guide to Drug Testing (2nd Ed.)	$9.95
Federal Manager's Guide to Total Quality Management	$9.95
Effective Writing for Feds	$9.95
Practical Ethics for the Federal Employee (2nd Ed.)	$9.95
Sexual Harassment and the Federal Employee (2nd Ed.)	$6.95
The Federal Manager's Guide to Preventing Sexual Harassment (2nd Ed.)	$9.95
The Federal Employee's Guide to EEO	$6.95
Federal Manager's Guide to Leave and Attendance (3rd Edition)	$9.95
The Ways of Wills	$14.95
Supervisor's Guide to Federal Labor Relations (3rd Edition)	$9.95
Welcome to the Federal Government	$6.95
Using Alternative Dispute Resolution in the Federal Government	$9.95
A Practical Guide to Using ADR in the Federal Service	$9.95
RIF's and Furloughs (2nd Ed.)	$14.95
Working Together: A Practical Guide to Partnerships	$9.95
A Practical Guide to Interest Based Bargaining	$9.95
Empowerment: A Practical Guide for Success	$9.95
Team Building: An Exercise in Leadership	$9.95
Managing Anger: Methods for a Happier and Healthier Life	$9.95
Dynamics of Diversity	$9.95
Voices of Diversity (hardback)	$22.95

PRACTITIONER PUBLICATIONS

The Desktop Guide to Unfair Labor Practices	$25.00
The Federal Employee's Law Practitioners Handbook	$59.95
The Federal Practitioner's Guide to Negotiability	$25.00
The Union Representative's Guide to Federal Labor Relations (2nd Ed.)	$9.95

The Federal Labor & Employee Relations Update
Subscription Fees   12 Months $225

The MSPB *Alert!*
Subscription Fees   12 Months $125
L&ER Update Subscribers pay only $95

The Federal EEO Update
Subscription Fees   1-9 Subscriptions $175 each

The Federal Manager's Edge
Subscription Fees

1-50 Subscriptions	$65 each
51-100 Subscriptions	$59 each
101-500 Subscriptions	$52 each
501-999 Subscriptions	$45 each
1000+ Subscriptions	$39 each

ELECTRONIC NEWSLETTERS

The Electronic Edge
Subscription Fees:
1. One year subscription: $200. This price includes one 3 1/2" floppy disk, one paper copy and the right to reproduce an unlimited number of copies to distribute throughout one organizational location.
2. Two year subscription: $375   3. Three year subscription: $510

The Electronic Federal Labor & Employee Relations Update
Subscription Fees:
1. One subscription: $595. This price includes one 3 1/2" disk, one paper copy and the right to reproduce an unlimited number of copies to distrib-ute throughout one organizational location.
2. Two year subscription: $1,095   3. Three year subscription: $1,510

The Electronic EEO Update
Subscription Fees:
1. One year subscription: $595. This price includes one 3 1/2" disk, one paper copy and the right to reproduce an unlimited number of copies to distribute throughout one organizational location.
2. Two year subscription: $1,095   3. Three year subscription: $1,510

FPMI Video Training Packages

PRICES EFFECTIVE THROUGH DECEMBER 31, 1997.

• Managing Cultural Diversity

Package includes 25 guidebooks with workshops; a facilitators handbook with suggested workshop answers and a script with techniques to conduct a training session on cultural diversity; master copies of vu-graphs; and a 28 minute video on implementing cultural diversity in your agency ($295 for the complete set).

• Dealing With Misconduct

Package includes video program, 25 guidebooks ($295).

• Writing Effective Performance Standards

Package includes video program, 25 guidebooks ($295).

• Managing Under a Labor Agreement
• Managing Under the Labor Relations Law

Order separate courses for $295 each. Special package includes both video programs with 25 workbooks for each course ($495).

• Sexual Harassment: Not Government Approved
• Preventing Sexual Harassment: Some Practical Answers

Order separate courses for $295 each. Or purchase our special package of both video programs with 25 workbooks and a leader's guide ($495).

• The FAIR™ Way To Manage Diversity

Package includes video program and 1 instructor's guide ($495).

Additional workbooks for each class are also available. Quantity discounts are also available on all tape purchases. Call for more information. (205) 539-1850.

• Resolving Labor Management Relations Issues Through Partnership

Includes 25 copies of the Participant's Workbook, one copy of the Instructor's Guide, 25 copies of *The Supervisor's Guide to Federal Labor Relations* and *The Union Representative's Guide to Federal Labor Relations*, plus master copies of overhead transparencies ($595).

• Practical Ethics Training for Government Managers and Employees

Includes 35 copies of the Participant's Workbook, 35 copies of *Practical Ethics for The Federal Employee*, one copy of the Instructor's Guide, and master copies of more than 50 black & white overhead transparencies ($595). Color transparencies and color slides available at additional cost.

• Effective Equal Employment Opportunity Leadership

Includes 25 copies of the Participant's Workbook, 25 copies of *The Federal Employee's Guide to EEO*, 25 copies of *The Federal Manager's Guide to EEO*, one copy of the Instructor's Guide, master copies of more than 50 black & white overhead transparencies ($595). Color transparencies and color slides available at additional cost.

**Please call for more information on these packages.
Quantity discounts available.
(205) 539-1850 or fax (205) 539-0911.**

FPMI Seminars

FPMI Communications, Inc. specializes in training seminars for federal managers and supervisors. These seminars can be conducted at your worksite at a flat rate that is substantially less than open enrollment seminars.

The instructors for FPMI seminars have all had practical experience with the federal government and know problems federal supervisors and employees face and how to deal effectively with those problems.

Some of the seminar-workshops available include:
- Building Productive Labor-Management Partnerships
- How To Use ADR and IBB
- Interest-Based Problem Solving
- Negotiating Labor Agreements Using Interest-Based Bargaining
- Negotiating Labor Agreements (Traditional)
- Pre-Retirement Seminar
- Taking Adverse and Performance-Based Actions
- Labor Relations for Supervisors
- Preventing Workplace Violence
- Resolving Organizational Conflict
- Managing the Dynamics of Organizational Change
- Making Discipline & Performance Decisions
- Managing Problem Employees Effectively
- RIF
- Developing Effective Performance Standards
- Developing Team-Based Performance Standards
- How to Review Performance with Employees
- Performance Management: New Rules, New Opportunities
- Working Together in a Diverse Workforce
- Preventing Sexual Harassment
- Effective Personnel Management for Supervisors & Managers
- How to Interview People Without Getting Fired, Demoted or Successfully Sued
- Effective Government Leadership in a Downsizing Environment
- How to Build an Effective Team in Your Agency
- Change Leadership for the '90's
- Handling ULP Disputes Effectively
- Preparing and Presenting Your Arbitration Case
- Practical Ethics and The Federal Employee
- Basic Labor Relations for Practitioners
- MSPB Advocacy
- Effective Legal Writing for Personnelists & EEO Officials
- Administrative Investigations and Report Writing
- Women in Management
- Time Management

For more information contact:
FPMI Communications, Inc.
707 Fiber Street
Huntsville, AL 35801-5833
PHONE (205) 539-1850
FAX (205) 539-0911
Email: fpmi@fpmi.com
Internet: http://www.fpmi.com